The River Cottage

Preserves Handbook

The River Cottage Preserves Handbook

by Pam Corbin

introduced by
Hugh Fearnley-Whittingstall

www.rivercottage.net

TEN SPEED PRESS
Berkeley

for my daughters,
Pip and Maddy

Originally published in slightly different form in Great Britain
by Bloomsbury Publishing Plc, London, in 2008

Grateful acknowledgment is made to Harper Collins Publishers Ltd. to reprint the beech leaf noyau
recipe from *Food for Free*. Copyright © 1972 by Richard Mabey. Reprinted by permission.

Library of Congress Cataloging-in-Publication Data is on file with the publisher.

ISBN: 978-1-58008-172-6

Printed in China

Design by willwebb.co.uk
Project editor: Janet Illsley

10 9 8 7 6 5 4 3 2 1

First U.S. Edition

Contents

I love jam

and all its jarred and bottled relatives, the extended family we call by the rather austere name *preserves*. Actually, they're not austere at all. They are warm, forward, and friendly, offering up both generous feisty flavors and intriguing spicy subtleties to all who embrace them.

Mostly, I love them for being so delicious. But I also cherish and admire them for something else. They epitomize the values at the heart of a well-run, contented kitchen. Firstly, they embody and thrive on seasonal abundance. Secondly, they are, or should be, intrinsically local, perfectly complementing the grow-your-own (or at least pick-your-own) philosophy. And thirdly, not to be sniffed at in these days of ecological anxiety, they are frugal, thrifty and parsimonious: they waste not, so we want not.

Jams, chutneys, and pickles embrace the seasons, but they also, in an elegant and entirely positive manner, defy them. They do so by stretching the bounty of more abundant months into the sparser ones. We shouldn't underestimate this achievement. Over the centuries, wizards and alchemists have used all the power and magic they can muster to try and catch rainbows, spin straw into gold, and even bring the dead back to life. They've failed, of course. Yet all the while, humble peasants and ordinary housewives have got on with the simple business of bottling sunshine so that it may spread a little joy in the leaner seasons . . . They call it jam.

More prosaically, I love the way that a couple of hours in the kitchen transforms a gardener's problem into a cook's delight. Come August and September, when it starts raining plums and you are wading through thigh-sized summer squash, your conscience would be rightly pricked if you threw such bounty on the compost heap. But when you know how to preserve your own fruit and vegetables, a glut of apples or a pile of pears becomes an exciting opportunity rather than a headache.

Yet I know many keen cooks, even some gardener cooks, who never make preserves. They love eating them, they love receiving them as gifts, they love the *idea* of making them, but something is holding them back. What is it? A fear, perhaps, of the perceived paraphernalia of jam making, a mild hysteria about the dangers of boiling sugar, a rumbling anxiety about the setting point. I know that such worries are unfounded – delusional even. So what can I do for these poor souls?

Well, I can introduce them to Pam Corbin. I first heard about "Pam the Jam" when she was running Thursday Cottage Preserves, a small commercial jam company that operated in an almost domestic way, making old-fashioned preserves the old-fashioned way, with real ingredients. When we started planning our Preserving Days at River Cottage, I knew Pam was the person for the job. She shares her passion and wealth of knowledge with enviable clarity and enthusiasm. Many of her sentences end with "it's simple, really," and with Pam to guide you, you really believe it is.

As this book has come together, my admiration for Pam has deepened. She is a great communicator who bestows infectious confidence on her charges. But more than that, she is a woman of decisive palate and impeccable good taste. Throughout the growing year that it took to produce this book, I was the lucky recipient of regular "jamograms" – little parcels of tasting pots of recipes that she was developing for the book.

From her early rhubarb jam to roasted sweet beet relish, and from apple lemon curd to roasted tomato ketchup, they were invariably exquisite. Your ambitions may be as modest as a few jars of perfect strawberry jam, but I'm quite confident that under Pam's guidance you will soon be dabbling with blackberry and apple leather, nasturtium "capers," figgy mostardo, and elixir of sage. Just writing their names makes me hungry.

Sadly, there wasn't room for all of Pam's fabulous recipes in this book. But it is a tribute to her remarkable gifts that every time we decided to leave one out, it felt like a minor tragedy. The upside is that every recipe that's in here is a tried-and-trusted gem. They met with universal approval from the River Cottage tasting panel – not a formal body, you understand, but a dangerous scrummage of whoever was around when Pam dropped by with a few more jars or bottles.

Pam's approach is not didactic, but encouraging and adventurous. Her message is that, once you've mastered a few basic techniques, there's really no stopping you. In this inspiring book, she will show you the ropes and then give you the reins. I'm absolutely sure you will enjoy the ride.

Hugh Fearnley-Whittingstall, Dorset, May 2008

Seasonality

Preserving the bounties of our fruitful summer and autumn

was normal – a way of life – not so many years ago. It was essential to stock up the larder for leaner months, when fresh food was scarce or unavailable and the sealed bottles and jars full of summer would help to allay the monotony of the winter diet. If soft summer currants and berries – and gluts of sweet-smelling tomatoes and baskets of vegetables – weren't *kept* in some form or another, then there would be no summer produce until the following year. There was no nipping down to the supermarket to buy, in the midst of January, a basket of strawberries or even a bag of tomatoes.

You don't need to turn the clock back far, just a couple of generations to the 1950s, when to own a home refrigerator or a freezer was considered opulent, and of course fresh foods didn't arrive each day of the week, each week of the year, by air and sea from all corners of the globe to flood shop shelves with produce that would otherwise be considered out of season.

The rationing of food in Britain that began during wartime finally finished in July 1954, nine years after the war had ended. The war years had seen the government allocating sugar to the Women's Institute (WI) for jam making so that surplus produce did not go to waste. The extent of food preservation by the WI did not stop at jam making; these resolute ladies also canned fruit and vegetables for the national food supply. The end to those long years of rationing coincided with an increase in the variety of imported foods readily available throughout the year. Unquestionably, for many this has meant that the structure and meaningful importance of working and living the seasons, along with the necessity to preserve and not waste, have vanished from everyday life.

Following the seasons

Food is never more flavorsome or as good as when it is fresh and in season, making the riches of a good harvest a just reward for anybody who is prepared to take notice of and be guided by the seasons. For me, there's not much to better a freshly dug new potato cooked up with a sprig of garden mint, and how these earthy roots can be thought of as humble is inexplicable, as they are a staple food worldwide. If stored correctly (dark and between 40° and 50°F), their firm and starchy bodies will keep naturally for months without any further action to preserve them.

Or, what could surpass devouring a plateful of freshly picked raspberries? These soft, juicy berries, however, will keep for barely a day or two before they begin to deteriorate, so action needs to be speedy to preserve them at their best. Raspberries are a wonderfully useful preserving ingredient, for they can be transformed into blissful jam, canned, turned into berry cordial, or used to make fruity vinegar, all to be put away and enjoyed later in the year.

By the very nature of the variable climate linked with each of the four seasons, much homegrown produce is available for limited periods, sometimes just a few swift weeks of the year, when crops of gluttish proportion are available to feast upon fresh and any surplus will be at its best preserved in some way or another. Ideally, produce to be preserved should be as fresh and local as possible, so every tasty scrap of its character is unmistakably captured. However, there are a few exceptions to the local rule, and until we see citrus groves swathing the land, the long-standing tradition of making marmalade to preserve the bitter Seville orange will continue, in addition to the use of tart, acidic lemon in all number of preserving and culinary recipes.

The familiarity of the pattern of the seasons and what each offers is fundamental to understanding how the preserving year is entwined with the growing seasons. The seasonal performance is undoubtedly the greatest show on earth: a perennial show in four parts, running for 365 days of the year with every month taking a worthy and significant role, where complementary ingredients brush shoulders at their growing time. You'll find that elderflowers add muscat perfume to gooseberries, pectin-rich red currants combine with low-pectin strawberries, and soft, fleshy apples partner seedy blackberries perfectly at autumn time.

The long slender stalks of rhubarb bridge the beginning and the end of each yearly cycle, starting around the time of the spring equinox, when the sun makes the first of its biannual crossings over the equator and the lengths of day and night are more or less equal. It is now that the first crinkled, sulfur-yellow rhubarb leaves begin to push their way up from the sleepy earth, unfurling to spread their towering umbrella leaves over silken red-green shoots. From here on, and until the quiescence of sleeping winter, there is usually something budding up and getting ready to yield some form of crop for us to harvest, so a sharp eye needs to be employed to avoid missing any of the seasonal gifts each month offers.

Spring

The spring months of April and May are the wake-up time, heralding the burst of new growth from latent pinkish-tinged buds and shoots that rapidly change into blossoms or velvety spring-green leaves. The feathery soft green foliage of the native beech begins to spill out from hedgerows in late April and early May, just ahead of the elderflowers, who run riot in a show-off way just about everywhere later in the month. Patches of nettles and wild garlic appear on sheltered banks, the tender young leaves just right to be turned into zesty pesto. Protected pockets of land will allow the first tiny green gooseberries of the season to be picked, and like the long red-green rhubarb stalks, these berries are sharp and tart too, almost as if it is nature's way of arousing our dulled taste buds, stimulating and preparing them for the rush of flavors to come. In preserving terms, these two months are still quite a lazy time, a teaser for the months ahead, but they are by no means idle. Use this time to check out your preserving gear (jars, bottles, lids, and things) and make sure your stocks of sugar, spices, and vinegar are plentiful for when the real season kicks off.

Summer

In June, we encounter the summer solstice, when the daylight hours are at their maximum and the increasing warmth gives rise to a frenzy of growing in all shapes and colors. We see the start of the soft fruit season with strings of shimmering red currants and the early varieties of strawberries and raspberries producing their first sweet berries. Aromatic herbs make themselves known, and their heady, sweet-smelling leaves can be used to augment vinegars and oils and to flavor pesto and relishes. The hedgerow shyly reveals diminutive silver-gray blackberry buds, while the petals of *Rosa canina* (dog rose) can be gathered to add fragrance to jams, jellies, cordials, and spirits. Down in the vegetable garden, the first fattening roots of sweet beets and the swollen heads of Florence fennel will be beginning to show.

July is the month when the wooden spoon begins to get busy. The early soft berries and currants of June extend to welcome main-crop varieties along with other currant and berry friends; black currants, blueberries, tayberries, and loganberries crop plentifully, and gooseberries reach sweet maturity to end their productive reign. The silver-gray blackberry buds of June break into pink-tinged white flowers, soon to metamorphose into the unmistakable drupelets of indigenous blackberries. Look closely at the elder bush and you'll see a mass of green underripe berries, which before long will glisten red-black as they ripen. Rosehips and hawthorn berries are like hedgerow chameleons, disguised in their leafy green coats before they first tinge bronze and then blush red for their autumnal show. Cherries, the first of the stone fruits, will be ready, but be quick – they won't last long, and eagle-eyed birds will be waiting to gorge upon them. Plums are beginning to swell, but it won't be until late in the month or the beginning of August that the early varieties of these orchard fruits will be ready.

August is the true glut month, when green beans, zucchini, tomatoes, cucumbers, and summer vegetables invariably oversupply, resulting in a glorious month to preserve as much as possible. The summer-fruiting raspberries are soon replaced by the first flush of blackberries – always the sweetest and juiciest of the year. Watch out for hanging clusters of scarlet rowans, the berries of the mountain ash, for these, combined with a handful of crab apples, will make an outstanding jelly of carnelian color.

Autumn

In September, you'll find your back step will become a home for refugee fruit, stuffed into bags and left by well-meaning friends who expect you to make all sorts of magnificent jams, jellies, and other preserves. As you try to make sure all is safely gathered before the cooler and shorter days of autumn set in, this month might seem a race against time. But don't panic, you'll find that summer squash, onions, apples, pears, and others have developed protective winter coats and, if carefully stored, will keep for a month or two, to use later in the year.

Orchard fruits will now be ripening. Plums, apples, and pears yield freely, ahead of the fragrant quince ready at the tail end of the month – watch out though, for too much moisture will make these golden beauties split. For wild food foragers, hedgerows are ablaze with color, intense with berries and fruits of all kinds; blackberries, rosehips, hawthorn berries, elderberries, scabby crab apples, and clusters of hazelnuts adorn native trees and bushes.

From here on, things really do begin to slow up. Much of the autumn harvest will be past its best. The woodland birds will have feasted well upon the hedgerow spread. Apples and pears are still plentiful to turn into Christmas mincemeat or spicy chutney, and onions pickled now will be just right for the festive season. Sweet chestnuts, split from spiky armor, can be found in heaps of fallen leaves, while raspberries, of the autumn kind, stretch berry-picking to this time.

Winter

As the year spins toward the winter solstice, the shorter, darkening days and the lack of sunlight hours allow the earth to rest from growing. The dormancy of the winter begins and only hardy leeks, blue-green brassicas, and a few rooty crops survive the cold. But still, within the cycle of the seasonal preserving year, there are two highlights yet to come. The bitter marmalade oranges from Seville arrive in early January, turning this month into a preserving stronghold of the year, when steamy citrus vapors fill our kitchens and larder shelves are replenished with jars of golden, amber, and tawny marmalade to last the year ahead.

Then finally, early rhubarb arrives to carry us through to the next perennial cycle. From late January to early March in darkened sheds and under tall forcing pots, the leaves force upward to boast the beauty of their slender, translucent pink stalks, heralding the start of another seasonal year.

The Rules

Preserving evokes deep-rooted, almost primeval feelings of self-sufficiency and survival, of gatherer and hunter, for this is how our ancestors stayed alive. These days, this all sounds more than a little extreme, but unquestionably a home with a good store of homemade preserves will generate a feeling of warmth and confidence.

I admit that at times I can get quite carried away thinking of how I can fill shapely jam jars, of the glistening grains of sugar, of the neroli-like perfume of Seville oranges . . . But I've also found that it pays to be aware of a small amount of cold, hard science, and to be familiar with some basic but important practical techniques. Once you understand why food goes bad, and how it can be prevented from doing so, your jam, jelly, and chutney making can reach new levels of success. Don't worry, you don't need a chemistry degree. . .

The simple fact is that any fresh food, unless it is treated in some way, will inevitably decay and become unsuitable for consumption. There are four meddlesome elements that cause spoilage in foods – enzymes, bacteria, molds/fungi, and yeasts – but if the cook intervenes to prevent or arrest their progress, most foods can be safely kept for extended periods of time.

The four spoilers

Microorganisms are generally viewed as undesirable, and if present in sufficient numbers, they make food a health hazard. In certain conditions, all microorganisms will flourish and increase. Some nonharmful microorganisms are deliberately brought into play in food production, of course – mold in blue cheeses, and yeasts in beer and bread making, for example – but it is the harmful microorganisms that concern us in preserves making.

Good food hygiene is the first step in stopping the spoilers. It is essential that all food be handled with care and all utensils, equipment, and work surfaces be spotlessly clean, so as few microorganisms as possible are present to start with.

The use of high temperatures is the second way to defeat the tricky foursome – hence, cooking is an integral part of many preserving processes. They may thrive in warmth, but they cannot take real heat.

High concentrations of sugar, acid, alcohol, or salt also kill these undesirables, or at the very least make it hard for them to flourish, and nearly all the preserving techniques in this book rely on large quantities of these ingredients to create conditions hostile to enzymes and microorganisms.

The final line of defense involves excluding the air these spoilers need to thrive. This is why well-sealed jars and bottles are essential, and why oil is another important preserving medium.

Enzymes

Enzymes are not actually organisms, but proteins found in all living things, animal or vegetable, and they perform a huge variety of roles. From a culinary point of view, it's important to know that enzymes remain active long after food has been harvested, and they function as catalysts for change, triggering and speeding up chemical processes. Enzymes trigger deterioration, for instance, by sparking off changes in tissue that in turn provide a fertile environment for the growth of microorganisms. The discoloring of cut or damaged fruit or vegetables is also caused by enzyme action. However, if the exposed surface comes into contact with an acid or alkali, the discoloration will slow down. This is why prepared produce is often rubbed with lemon juice or plunged into lightly salted water.

Enzymes increase their activity at temperatures between 84° and 122°F and will begin to be destroyed at temperatures above 140°F. Their action is also halted at temperatures below freezing but will increase again when warmth returns.

Bacteria

So small that they are only visible under a microscope, bacteria are the most ancient and widespread form of life on earth. Bacteria increase rapidly at temperatures between 68° and 104°F. They become dormant in the freezer and are destroyed at or near 212°F – the boiling point of water. Bacterial spoilage of food is sometimes difficult to detect, and although most bacteria are harmless – some even useful – some cause food to rot and become foul smelling, and their toxins are harmful to health. It is therefore vital not to take any shortcuts with preserving procedures, and to follow all instructions carefully to avoid any form of bacterial contamination.

Molds and fungi

The spores of molds and fungi are present in the air around us and will take root in almost any food. Initially, they produce fine threads, then the characteristic gray-green, cottony bloom. Molds and fungi are dormant at 32°F and thrive at temperatures between 50° and 100°F, and their spoiling activities decrease from 140° to 190°F, which is why cooking is an efficient way to get rid of them. A bit of mold on the top of an open jar of jam should not be scooped off and ignored; as they grow, some molds produce mycotoxins that can be harmful if eaten.

Yeasts

The yeasts found in foods are generally not harmful to health but can cause spoilage. Most species are quickly destroyed at 140°F and above and are inactivated by cold. Some grow in food containing as much as 60 percent sugar, and badly covered or half-used jars of jam stored in a warm kitchen are prime sites for yeasts to begin to ferment. The gases produced may cause the preserve to pop when the lid is removed.

Potting, packing, and sealing

Proper potting and sealing is one of the main pillars of good preserves making. If done incorrectly, it can ruin a batch of otherwise perfect preserves. These days, some form of glass vessel with a secure seal is generally used. To reduce the risk of bacterial contamination, it is important to sterilize the container and fully fill or "jam-pack" it with your preserves.

Sterilizing jars

Any microorganism lurking in the container you put your preserves into has the potential to grow and contaminate, which is why it is essential to use sterile jars. There are three simple ways to sterilize jars: you can immerse them in a pan of water and bring to a boil; wash them in very hot and soapy water, rinse thoroughly, then dry them in a very low oven; or simply put them through a hot dishwasher cycle.

Whichever method you choose, only clean the jars shortly before they are to be used and make sure they are dry. This minimizes the time in which the jars might pick up new contaminants. Also, all hot preserves should be poured into warm jars (this helps to prevent the temperature from dropping before the seal is applied), so you might as well use them before they have cooled down from the drying process.

Reusing jars and bottles

I like to reuse jars and bottles whenever possible. As well as keeping costs down, it gives me a wide variety of shapes and sizes to choose from. However, reused jars should always be cleaned both inside and outside, then very carefully examined to make sure they are not damaged in any way. Cracks or chips are ideal breeding grounds for bacteria and can also shed tiny splinters of glass that could cause injury if swallowed.

Old labels on reused jars should be fully removed. I find the best way of attacking this job is to fully immerse the jars in a pan of cold water, bring to a simmer, and simmer for 10 minutes. I then let the jars cool and, when cool enough to handle, rub off the label with the blunt side of a knife. Tamper-resistant seals and labels on lids can be removed in the same way.

If you do want to buy jars, they are available from specialty shops and are generally sold in certain sizes that comply with the requirements for commercially produced preserves. If you are using an assortment of old jars, you can measure their capacity in volume (just fill them with water, then pour the water into a measuring cup).

Jar sizes

Before you start making preserves, you should check the recipe to see how many jars you will need so you can have them ready. Thankfully, almost all jars share just two or three lid sizes, so lids can often be mixed and matched between various jars and bottles.

Sealing jars

Having packed your preserves, the next vital thing is to seal the jars as quickly as possible to prevent entry of oxygen and airborne microorganisms. For hot sweet preserves, chutneys, and relishes, this can be done with a twist-on lid. Pickles and vinegar preserves should always be sealed with vinegar-proof twist-on lids.

I like to seal fruit cheeses by pouring melted food-grade paraffin wax over the surface, giving a really traditional finish to the filled pots. The easiest way to melt the wax is to place it in a heatproof bowl (I keep one especially for this) and stand it in a pan of gently simmering water until the wax is liquid.

Twist-on lids The metal twist-on lids that come with most jars are very easy to use and create a good tight seal. Generally, these days, most lids have a plasticized lining that is suitable for use with both sugar- and vinegar-based preserves. Avoid the use of unlined metal lids with vinegar preserves because they will corrode and spoil the preserves. For the best possible results, I recommend always using new lids, even with reused jars. Previously used lids are still an option, but you must make sure they are not damaged in any way and they should be sterilized by boiling in a pan of water for 10 minutes before use.

Bottles

I stash away old bottles of various shapes and sizes to use when making cordials, fruit liqueurs, and flavored vinegars and oils. Vinegar bottles with twist-on lids are excellent for flavored vinegars, cordials, and fruit syrups, while small, interesting-shaped spirit bottles are jolly useful for fruit liqueurs and make attractive gifts.

A good range of bottles can be purchased from specialty shops, including old-fashioned preserving bottles with a swing-top lid fastening. I particularly like using these nice-looking bottles; made from toughened glass, they are easy to use, the lid is attached, and they can be used time and time again. All bottles, lids, and corks should be sterilized by boiling for 10 minutes in a pan of water before use.

Filling and sealing

Careful potting and sealing at the correct temperature for the particular preserve is important for the keeping quality.

TYPE OF PRESERVE	TEMPERATURE	NOTES
Jams, jellies, fruit butters and cheeses, and marmalades	Hot fill (preserves should be above 185°–194°F) warm, dry jars, to within ¹/₈ inch of the rim.	Allow whole fruit jams and chunky marmalades to stand for 10–15 minutes after cooking, before putting into jars.
Fruit curds	Fill warm jars as soon as the curd is cooked.	Because curd is poured at a lower temperature than jam, ensure it is sealed as quickly as possible.
Chutneys, relishes, sauces, and ketchups	Hot fill warm, dry jars.	Remove air pockets by sharply tapping the jars. Use vinegar-proof lids. Some sauces may need to be sterilized in a water bath (see p. 156).
Pickles and sweet pickles	Hot or cold fill clean, dry jars to within ¹/₄ inch of the rim.	Use vinegar-proof lids. Remove air pockets by sharply tapping the jars.
Fruit syrups	Hot fill clean bottles and seal immediately.	To extend shelf life, sterilize in a water bath or an oven (see pp. 156–58).
Canned fruits	It is essential to follow individual recipes precisely.	See Canned Fruits (pp. 150–77).
Oil- and alcohol-based preserves	Cold fill. Make sure ingredients are totally immersed before sealing.	Remove air pockets by sharply tapping jars. Seal with a twist-on lid.

Labeling

Use self-adhesive labels with plenty of space to record what the preserve is and when it was made. Plain labels can be used, but there are lots of attractive labels on the market designed especially for preserves making. If you're adept on the computer, you can even design your own. Don't try to stick a label on a hot jar – the glue will melt and it will fall off. Wait until jars are cold before labeling.

Safekeeping

Preserves with a good seal should last a long time, although the texture and color may well deteriorate. Nonetheless, I'd be the first to admit that a murky jar of some old concoction discovered during a larder clear-out will have little appeal – and there is always an underlying concern that it might have gone bad. The chart below contains guidelines for safekeeping and pleasant eating. (Chutneys, pickles, and marmalades, by the way, improve with a maturing period so shouldn't be eaten straight away.)

Once preserves are opened, look after them. Replace lids securely and keep the preserves in a cool place because, once the seal on a jar or bottle is broken, the contents are vulnerable and can be recontaminated by microorganisms.

PRESERVE	IDEAL SHELF LIFE
Fruit curds	Use within 4 weeks and refrigerate once opened.
Vegetables in oil	Use within 4 months. Refrigerate once opened and use within 6 weeks.
Pesto	Refrigerate and use within 4 weeks.
Fruit butters	Use within 9 months and refrigerate once opened.
Jams and jellies	Use within 1 year.
Fruit cheeses	Use within 1 year and refrigerate once opened.
Mincemeat	Use within 1 year.
Relishes	Use within 1 year and refrigerate once opened.
Sauces	Use within 1 year.
Chutneys and pickles	Store for 4–10 weeks before using. Use within 1–2 years.
Marmalades	Use within 2 years.
Alcohol preserves	Use within 3 years.

In a cool, dry, dark place These conditions apply to the storage of all preserves. Few houses these days have good old-fashioned larders or cellars, so you may find the best place to keep your preserves is in the garage or shed.

Key preserving ingredients

Most of the ingredients needed for preserving are in general use in a busy kitchen. It is, however, worth considering their different characteristics.

Sugar

A concentration of over 60 percent sugar in preserves creates an environment that is hostile to microorganisms. Sugar can also be combined with vinegar in sweet-and-sour preserves such as chutneys and sauces. The sugar you use not only affects the cooking process, but also influences the final flavor of your preserves.

Granulated sugar Available in pure white or golden, unrefined varieties, this is a good basic, inexpensive sugar that will work well in almost any of the recipes in this book. It has medium-coarse grains, so it takes a little longer to dissolve than superfine sugar but is less likely to stick to the bottom of the pan and burn. Granulated sugar is produced from sugar beets, but an intensive refining process is involved. If you'd prefer an unrefined sugar, which will retain its natural golden color and delicate caramel flavor, choose one derived from sugarcane. I use both unrefined and refined granulated sugar. Unrefined sugar is ideal for marmalades and with strong-flavored fruits such as black currants, but I prefer a refined white sugar for more delicate fruits and berries, for jellies and curds, and for flavored liqueurs.

Coarse sugar This is more costly than granulated sugar. It's by no means essential for good preserves, but the big, chunky crystals dissolve slowly, need less stirring, and are less likely to stick to the bottom of the pan. They also produce less froth or scum.

Brown sugar Using unrefined Demerara or muscovado sugar in a jam or chutney – either wholly or in combination with a lighter sugar – changes the color and taste. These dark sugars are not highly processed and are full of natural molasses flavor. They can overpower delicate ingredients but are wonderful when used with citrus fruit in marmalades or with vinegar and spices in savory chutneys and pickles.

Honey This can be used to add another layer of flavor to preserves, although it cannot entirely replace the sugar as it burns very easily. Replace 10 to 15 percent of the total sugar in a recipe with honey and add it when the sugar has dissolved.

Vinegar

Vinegar has been used for centuries to preserve everything from onions to eggs, and foods preserved in this medium are generally referred to as being pickled. The word *vinegar* comes from the medieval French *vin-aigre*, meaning "sour wine." It is produced by a double fermentation of some form of fruit or grain. The first fermentation is brought about by yeasts turning sugar into alcohol, as in the production of wine, beer, and cider. The second fermentation involves bacteria turning the alcohol into acetic acid, thereby creating vinegar.

In order to preserve successfully, the acetic acid content of vinegar must be at least 5 percent – check the label. This level of acidity creates an environment in which few microorganisms can survive. The harsh flavor of vinegar can be mitigated by the addition of sugar and/or spices, while the choice of vinegar itself will also have a considerable effect on the final taste of your pickles.

Malt vinegar Produced from fermented barley, malt vinegar is inexpensive and has been the backbone of traditional pickling for many years. It has a very strong taste that some people love, but I often find it a bit too aggressive. Nevertheless, in a really hearty, well-spiced chutney or pickle, it can give precisely the right robust bass note of flavor, and it's a stalwart favorite for pickled onions. The color in dark malt vinegar comes from the addition of caramel – pure, distilled malt vinegar is colorless.

Wine vinegars Derived from grapes, red and white wine vinegars are more expensive than malt vinegar but have a finer, more delicate flavor. I like to use them for pickling ingredients such as nasturtium pods, where I don't want the pods' fiery bite swamped by vinegar.

Cider vinegar This is sweeter and fruitier than wine vinegar and my choice for seasonal chutneys, pickles, and relishes. Specialty stores sell an excellent range of cider vinegars, and if you live in cider apple country, you may well find some excellent local varieties.

Salt

High concentrations of salt are, of course, inimical to yeast, bacteria, and molds, which is why this ingredient is so important in many preserving methods. Salt is also crucial for enhancing flavor. In addition, it is often used in the preparation of foods prior to pickling, where it draws out excess water, which would otherwise dilute and spoil the preserves (see Pickles, Chutneys & Relishes, beginning on p. 84).

Sea salt This is produced by evaporating seawater. You can buy unrefined, natural flaky types, such as Maldon or Halen Môn, which are lovely sweet-tasting ingredients. They are also much more expensive than other salts, so while you might be happy to use them for seasoning, you may think it rather extravagant to use them in large quantities for dry-salting or pickling. A relatively inexpensive fine-grained sea salt, available from health food stores or supermarkets, is what I use most often in preserving. It's certainly the most suitable type for dry-salting vegetables for pickling, as it will coat them well. However, like many fine-grained, free-flowing salts, some fine sea salts contain an anticaking agent, so do check labels before you buy.

Rock salt Generally the cheaper alternative to sea salt, this is mined from underground mineral deposits. It may also be sold as kitchen salt or table salt. Some are highly processed, purified, and treated and taste correspondingly harsh. I don't use salts like this in preserving, as they can affect the final quality of the preserves. However, coarse, additive-free rock salts are available and make a good alternative to sea salt.

Alcohol

Alcohol is a very useful preserving medium, but to function effectively, it must be in the form of a spirit that is at least 40 percent alcohol (80 proof). Gin, vodka, rum, brandy, and whiskey are all suitable. Gin is a tried-and-tested favorite with fruits such as damson plums, while pitted cherries will make a splendid liqueur when steeped in brandy. Colorless eau-de-vie (brandy or flavorless alcohol that has not been aged) is an ideal base for more delicate or subtle ingredients. Wines, fortified wines, and cider can be used for preserving but need to be combined with other preservative ingredients, such as sugar, or with sterilizing methods, such as canning.

Oil

An effective means of sealing out oxygen, oil is a useful and potentially delicious part of many savory preserves. The oil will be an integral part of the finished preserves, and as it will have taken on flavor from the preserved food, you might want to use it to enhance other dishes. So I'd advise always using the best you can afford.

Olive oil This is extracted by grinding olives to a paste and then pressing with large millstones. Extra-virgin refers to olive oil with very low acidity, which is completely unrefined and taken from the first pressing of the olives. It's considered to be the very best type. However, it is expensive and often powerfully flavored, and I rarely use it in preserves. Virgin olive oil has a little more acidity but is also unrefined and will have a good flavor. It is much more affordable and is my choice for most oil-based preserves. Anything labeled "pure" olive oil, or just "olive oil," will be a blend of refined and unrefined oils. Less exciting, they are still perfectly acceptable to use.

Sunflower oil Light in color, almost flavorless, and much less expensive than olive oil, a good-quality sunflower oil is useful when you don't want the taste of the oil to intrude on the preserves. It can also be blended with other, more robustly flavored oils (see below).

Canola oil Golden in color and nutty in flavor, this is extracted from the tiny, jet-black seeds of *Brassica napus*, a member of the mustard family. It contains less saturated fat than any other oil, is high in omega-3s, and is a good source of vitamin E. I like to use it for flavored oils.

Hempseed oil Cold-pressed hempseed oil is vivid green in color and has a very strong nutty flavor. Alone, it would be overpowering for many ingredients, but 10 to 15 percent blended with sunflower oil creates a well-flavored oil.

Equipment for preserving

Equipping yourself for preserving will not entail a second mortgage. You probably already have most of the equipment you need in your kitchen. Here is a very quick run-through of essentials and useful items.

Preserving pan This is almost an essential item – but a large, wide, heavy-bottomed stockpot could stand in. Preserving pans do have the advantages of sloping sides, which maximize evaporation, a pouring lip, and a strong carrying handle. Go for a robust stainless steel preserving pan with a capacity of about 9 quarts. This should be large enough for most jamming and chutney sessions. Your pan must be deep enough to contain the rapid rise in liquid that occurs when jam comes to a full rolling boil. It is useful to buy one with a calibrated volume measure on the inside of the pan, which allows you to see by how much your ingredients have reduced.

Wooden spoons These need to be big and long handled. If possible, keep one especially for jam and one for chutney making (they will become impregnated with fruity and vinegary juices respectively).

Candy thermometer This is not expensive and will help you to check that your preserves have reached the right temperature for setting up, as well as giving you an accurate guide to temperature when canning.

Slotted spoon For skimming scum or fishing out fruit pits.

Sieves A couple of sieves are useful for puréeing fruit.

Paper coffee filters For straining small quantities of fruit vinegar or liqueur.

Food mill Great laborsaving tool for puréeing fruits and removing skins and seeds simultaneously. Useful when making fruit butters and cheeses.

Jelly strainer bag, or cheesecloth, and stand These are essential for straining the juice from cooked fruit when making jellies. Purpose-made jelly strainer bags and stands are available from specialty shops. Or you can improvise, using an upturned stool with a double thickness of cheesecloth tied to each leg to form a bag. Jelly strainer bags and cheesecloth can be reused, even though they become stained by fruit dyes. Before use (even when new), they should be scalded by placing in a pan of water and bringing to a boil.

Spice infuser Not essential, but an alternative to tying spices in cheesecloth for spicing vinegars and chutneys.

Measuring cups and spoons One or two calibrated, heat-resistant measuring cups are indispensable for measuring ingredients and pouring preserves into jars. A set of measuring spoons is also very useful for spices and seasonings.

Funnel A wide-necked pouring funnel can prevent spillages when filling jars but is not essential – a steady hand and a good pouring pitcher are often easier.

Accurate kitchen scales Very important for preserving success.

Jams & Jellies

This is the sweetest chapter in the book, where you will meet what I call the "sugar set" – in other words, recipes that rely purely on a high concentration of sugar to keep spoiling at bay. Sugar-based recipes form a broad and extensive branch of the preserving tree, and they are also the most familiar and perhaps widely used type of preserves. Here you will find out just how essential sugar is as a preserving ingredient and how, by means of various preserving techniques, it can be used to transform a host of fresh produce into goodies that can be safely stored away for the future. The different types of sugar-based preserves that I make at home are as follows.

Jams Without doubt, jams are the most familiar of all the sweet preserves. They are simply mixtures of lightly softened fruit and sugar, boiled together until they gel into a mass.

Marmalades Although originally referring to a type of quince jam (*marmelo* being the Portuguese word for quince), the term *marmalade* is now universally understood to mean a bittersweet preserve made from citrus fruit. Marmalades are made in a similar way to jams, but the hard citrus peel needs long, slow cooking to soften it before sugar is added.

Conserves Made with whole fruit that has been steeped in sugar before cooking to draw out the juices, a conserve is similar to a jam but often has a slightly softer set. Commercially, the word *conserve* is often used to describe a posh jam with a high fruit content.

Fruit spreads and fridge jams These are relatively low in sugar and usually made with added pectin to help them set. In general, they still have a softer, looser set than traditional jams. Providing they are sealed when still over 195°F, they will keep for 9 to 12 months. However, once opened, they must be kept in the fridge as they do not contain sufficient sugar to prevent them from spoiling at cool larder temperature.

Jellies Clear, translucent, and smooth (no fruity bits), fruit jellies are the jewels of the pantry. They are made by boiling strained fruit juice with sugar. They are best made with fruits high in both pectin and acid, such as apples, crab apples, gooseberries, and red currants – either on their own or in combination with other, lower-pectin fruits (see the pectin and acid content chart on p. 40). The basic fruit juice and sugar mixture can also be used as a base for herb or flower jellies.

Fruit butters So called because they spread as soft as butter, these are made by boiling cooked, sieved fruit pulp with sugar. They are lower in sugar than traditional jams and will not keep as well. For this reason, they are best potted in smallish jars, which can be consumed in a relatively short time, and stored in the fridge once opened.

Fruit cheeses These dense, solid preserves are similar to fruit butters in that they are made by boiling sieved fruit pulp with sugar. However, they are cooked for longer and taste richer and fruitier. You could make a cheese with almost any fruit, but because of the large quantity required, recipes usually favor prolific orchard, stone, and hedgerow fruits, such as apples, quince, damson plums, or crab apples. Fruit cheeses are normally packed in straight-sided jars or molds so the preserves can be turned out whole and sliced.

Fruit curds These are not true preserves, being very low in sugar, but creamy mixtures of butter, eggs, sugar, and an acidic fruit pulp or juice. To prevent the eggs from curdling, they are cooked very gently in a double boiler or in a bowl over a pan of boiling water. Curds are best eaten within 3 to 4 weeks, so they are usually made in fairly small quantities.

Mincemeats Again, these are not true sugar preserves, as alcohol plays its part in the process too. Mincemeats are mixtures of dried fruit, apples, spices, citrus zest, sugar, suet (sometimes), and alcohol. They are traditionally made in the autumn when the new season's apples are crisp and juicy, then kept for a couple of months to mellow and mature in time to make mince pies for Christmas.

Fruit leathers These rely on drying, as well as sugar, to preserve the fruit. A lightly sweetened purée is slowly dried in a low oven (or, in suitable climates, under the sun), producing a thin, pliable sheet. Fruit leathers store well for several months.

Candied fruits This is a generic term for fruits preserved by being steeped in sugar for a period of time. The sugar penetrates the fruit flesh, replacing some of the natural juices. Different types include glacé fruits, which are coated with a clear sugar syrup, and crystallized fruits, which are rolled in grains of sugar.

The essential foursome

In jam, jelly, and marmalade making, four ingredients are necessary to produce the magic result known as a set – i.e., the right wobbling, spreadable consistency. These are fruit, pectin, acid, and sugar. Getting to know them will help to ensure success.

Fruit

All fruit for preserves making should be dry, as fresh as possible, and slightly under-ripe. Overripe, wet fruit contains less pectin and acid and makes poor-quality preserves. If you find yourself snowed under with produce during a particularly good cropping season, remember that most fruits, including Seville oranges, can be frozen and used later in the year quite successfully. Bear in mind that the pectin content reduces a little with freezing, so sometimes extra pectin may need to be added.

With the exception of the citrus family, I like to use local fruits in the recipes for this chapter. There are, of course, a whole host of imported exotics at our disposal these days, but buying these in the quantities required for jam making can be expensive. In any case, with the abundance of homegrown fruits available to us, it's hardly necessary.

Pectin

Pectin is a natural substance found in all fruit (and some vegetables) in varying quantities (see the fruit pectin and acid content chart on p. 40). When combined with acid and sugar, it takes on a gumlike consistency – which is why it's essential in achieving a good set. Concentrated in cores, pith, skins, and seeds, it is released from the cell walls as the fruit is cooked. Pectin levels are at their highest in slightly underripe fruit and will decrease as the fruit ripens, or if it is frozen.

Fruit with lots of pectin will produce a jam or jelly that sets easily, while those containing lower amounts may well need a bit of help. This can come from other high-pectin fruits added to the mix (as with blackberry and apple jelly, for instance). Alternatively, extra pectin can be added in the form of a pectin stock (see p. 39) or commercially produced liquid or powdered pectin (usually extracted from apples or citrus fruit).

> How to test for pectin If you follow the chart on p. 40, you shouldn't need to test for pectin. However, if you're using a fruit not covered here, there is a simple way to check the pectin levels. Add 1 teaspoon of the cooked fruit juice to 1 tablespoon denatured alcohol (or gin or whiskey, as these work too). Shake gently and leave for a minute or two. Juice from a pectin-rich fruit will form a firm clot. If the juice forms several small clots, this indicates a medium pectin content. Juice that remains fairly liquid signifies a low pectin level.

Homemade pectin stock A pectin-rich stock is easily made from certain fruits. The procedure is much the same as the early stages of jelly making.

Combine 2 pounds 4 ounces red currants, gooseberries, or coarsely chopped (but not peeled or cored) sour cooking apples with 2 cups of water. Bring to a simmer and cook gently for 45 minutes to 1 hour, until the fruit is soft. Strain through a jelly strainer bag (see p. 33). The resulting pectin stock will keep for up to 4 weeks in the fridge. To keep it longer, either freeze it (but allow for a reduction in strength when using) or sterilize it.

To sterilize, bring the juice to a boil; pour into hot, sterilized preserving jars; and seal immediately. Immerse the jars in a pan of hot water with a folded tea towel on the bottom. Heat the water until boiling, then boil for 5 minutes. Remove the jars carefully and store in a cool, dry place.

To use the stock, stir $4^1/2$ to 9 tablespoons of it (depending on the fruit) into every pound of low-pectin, softened fruit before sugar is added.

FRUIT	PECTIN	ACID
Apples (cooking)	HIGH	HIGH
Apples (crab)	HIGH	HIGH
Apples (dessert)	MEDIUM	LOW
Apricots	MEDIUM	LOW
Blackberries (early)	MEDIUM	LOW
Blackberries (late)	LOW	LOW
Blueberries	MEDIUM	HIGH
Cherries (sour)	MEDIUM	HIGH
Cherries (sweet)	LOW	LOW
Citrus fruit	HIGH	HIGH
Currants (red, black, and white)	HIGH	HIGH
Damson plums	HIGH	HIGH
Elderberries	LOW	LOW
Figs	LOW	LOW
Gooseberries	HIGH	HIGH
Loganberries	MEDIUM	HIGH
Mulberries	MEDIUM	HIGH
Peaches	LOW	LOW
Pears	LOW	LOW
Plums (sour)	HIGH	HIGH
Plums (sweet)	MEDIUM	MEDIUM
Quince	HIGH	LOW
Raspberries (ripe)	MEDIUM	MEDIUM
Raspberries (unripe)	MEDIUM	LOW
Rhubarb	LOW	LOW
Rowanberries	MEDIUM-LOW	HIGH
Strawberries	LOW	LOW

Acid

Acid is naturally found in fruit and is essential for clear, bright, well-set preserves. It draws pectin out of the fruit, enabling the setting point to be reached quickly without lengthy cooking, which would darken the jam. Acid also helps prevent crystallization of the sugar. Levels of acid vary in different fruits (see chart, p. 40) and are lower in overripe fruit. Lemon, gooseberry, or red currant juice is sometimes added to low-acid fruit jams. It should be added before the fruit is cooked, so it can get to work on drawing out the pectin. If you're making jam with a low-acid fruit, such as strawberries or rhubarb, add 1 tablespoon of lemon juice, or $4^1/_2$ tablespoons of red currant, gooseberry, or apple juice, per pound of fruit.

Sugar

Sugar is the fourth vital ingredient for jam making and the one that actually preserves the fruit and keeps it from spoiling. In order to do this, the proportion of sugar in preserves needs to be 60 percent or higher. Boiling the fruit and sugar mixture drives off water, which helps the sugar content reach this crucial level. Sugar also enhances the flavor of sharp, acidic fruits such as black currants and gooseberries. See Key preserving ingredients, p. 27, for in-depth information on different types of sugar.

Setting point

Providing the proportion of ingredients is correct, your jam or jelly should set once it has been sufficiently cooked. There are three simple methods you can use to check if the setting point has been reached. Remove the jam from the heat while testing (it will lose water as it cooks and may then set too firmly). If the setting point has not been reached, return to a boil, cook for a further couple of minutes, then test again.

Crinkle or saucer test Drop a little jam onto a cold saucer (I put one in the fridge when I start making jam). Allow to cool for a minute, then push gently with your fingertip. If the jam crinkles, the setting point has been reached.

Dollop test Dip a clean wooden spoon into the jam, hold it up over the pan, twirl it around a couple of times, then let the jam drop from the side of it. If the jam doesn't run freely off the spoon but falls away in small dollops, the setting point has been reached.

Temperature test Place a candy thermometer (see p. 33) into the jam when it has reached a rolling boil. When it reads 220°F, the setting point has been reached. Pectin-rich fruits will set a degree or two lower.

Making perfect jams and marmalades

This checklist will help to ensure success every time:

1. Always use fresh, dry, slightly underripe fruit. Prepare and pick over according to type; i.e., hull strawberries, pit plums, top and tail gooseberries, shred citrus peel. Wash the fruit only if necessary and dry it well.

2. Simmer the fruit gently in a large, uncovered pan before adding the sugar. This softens the fruit and helps draw out the pectin. Soft fruits, such as raspberries and strawberries, will not need added water, but tougher-skinned or semihard fruits, such as currants, gooseberries, plums, apples, and citrus fruit, will.

3. Make sure that the fruit skins are well softened before sugar is added. Once the sugar is in, the skins will not soften further, no matter how long you cook them. Citrus peel for marmalade takes 1½ to 2 hours to soften.

4. Adding a little butter or cooking oil (2 teaspoons per pound of fruit) at the same time as the sugar helps prevent any scum from forming.

5. After adding the sugar to the fruit or juice, stir it over gentle heat to ensure it is completely dissolved before the mixture begins to boil. Adding the sugar before the jam boils helps to hold the fruit in whole or chunky pieces. Warming the sugar in a low oven will speed up the dissolving process but is not strictly necessary.

6. Once the sugar is dissolved, cook the jam, without stirring, at a full rolling boil, i.e., when the surface is covered by a mass of foamy bubbles that don't recede when stirred. Time your cooking from the point at which the rolling boil begins. Don't stir at this stage – it cools the jam, so it would take longer to reach the setting point.

7. Test for the setting point, using one of the methods given on p. 41, when the foamy bubbles have subsided and the surface of the boiling jam appears glossy and heavy.

8. When the setting point is reached, remove the pan from the heat. To remove scum, stir the jam (always in the same direction so as not to introduce too much air) until it has dispersed. Alternatively, skim off scum with a slotted spoon. (Scum, by the way, is nothing to worry about – it's just air bubbles created by the intense cooking process.)

9. Allow jams with large pieces of fruit and thick-cut marmalades to cool for 10 to 12 minutes before potting. This allows the mixture to thicken slightly so that the fruit, when potted, should remain well distributed throughout the jar.

10. Pour into clean, sterilized jars (see p. 21) while the preserves are still very hot (always above 185°F). Seal with suitable lids and, once cool, store in a cool, dry place.

Making perfect jellies

You will need to prepare the fruit in the same way as for jams (see left), but there are different watchpoints for jelly making:

1. Soften the fruit by simmering it very gently for 45 to 60 minutes. With juicy fruits, like strawberries, raspberries, red currants, and blackberries, allow $^1/_2$ to $^2/_3$ cup of water per pound of fruit. For plums, allow 1 cup per pound, and for black currants $1^1/_2$ cups per pound. Apples, quince, and hard fruits should be just covered with water.

2. Strain the cooked fruit pulp through a jelly strainer bag (see p. 33) for at least 2 hours or overnight; this helps make the jelly clear.

3. If you can't resist squeezing or poking the bag to extract more juice, be prepared for your jelly to be cloudy.

4. Allow 1 pound of sugar for every 3 cups of juice. Bring the juice slowly to a boil and add the sugar only when boiling. This helps to keep your jelly clear and bright; the longer the sugar is cooked, the more the jelly will darken. Boiling time will be somewhere between 5 and 15 minutes, depending on the type of fruit used.

5. Test for the setting point in the same way as for jam (see p. 41).

6. Skim the jelly and pour into jars as quickly as possible.

Seville orange marmalade

Season: mid-January to February

The bitter Seville orange is the most traditional and arguably the finest marmalade fruit of all. Only available for a few short weeks starting in mid-January, this knobbly, often misshapen orange has a unique aromatic quality and is very rich in pectin. However, you can use almost any citrus fruit to make good marmalade – consider sweet oranges, blood oranges, grapefruit, limes, clementines, kumquats, or a combination of two or three (see my suggested variations on p. 46).

There are two basic ways of making marmalade. My first choice is the sliced fruit method, which involves cutting the raw peel into shreds before cooking. I find this technique produces a brighter, clearer result. However, the whole fruit method, in which the fruit is boiled whole before being cut up, is easier and less time-consuming. It tends to create a darker, less delicate preserve – but that, of course, might be exactly what you want. I've given you both methods here.

Sliced fruit method

Makes five to six 12-ounce jars
2^1/$_4$ pounds Seville oranges
^{1}/$_3$ cup lemon juice
10 cups Demerara sugar

Scrub the oranges, remove the buttons at the top of the fruit, then cut in half. Squeeze out the juice and keep to one side. Using a sharp knife, slice the peel, pith and all, into thin, medium, or chunky shreds, according to your preference. Put the sliced peel into a bowl with the orange juice and cover with 10 cups of water. Let soak overnight or for up to 24 hours.

Transfer the whole mixture to a preserving pan, bring to a boil, then simmer slowly, covered, until the peel is tender. This should take approximately 2 hours, by which time the contents of the pan will have reduced by about one-third.

Stir in the lemon juice and sugar. Bring the marmalade to a boil, stirring until the sugar has dissolved. Boil rapidly until the setting point is reached (see p. 41), 20 to 25 minutes. Remove from the heat. Let cool for 8 to 10 minutes – a little longer if the peel is in very chunky pieces – then stir gently to disperse any scum. Pour into warm, sterilized jars and seal immediately (see pp. 21–22). Use within 2 years.

Whole fruit method

Makes five 12-ounce jars
2^1/$_4$ pounds Seville oranges
^{1}/$_3$ cup lemon juice
10 cups granulated sugar

Scrub the oranges, remove the buttons at the top, and put the whole oranges into a preserving pan with 10 cups of water. Bring to a boil, then simmer, covered, for 2 to 2½ hours, until the orange skins are tender and can be pierced easily with a fork.

When cool enough to handle, take the oranges out. Measure and keep the cooking water – you should have about 7 cups. Bring it up to this amount with more water if you have less, or boil to reduce if you have more.

Cut the oranges in half and remove the seeds with a fork, flicking them into a bowl. Strain any juice from the seeds back into the cooking water, then discard the seeds.

Meanwhile, cut up the orange peel and flesh into thick, medium, or thin shreds. Put the cut-up fruit into the strained cooking liquid. Add the lemon juice and sugar and bring to a boil, stirring until the sugar has completely dissolved. Bring to a rolling boil and boil rapidly until the setting point is reached (see p. 41), 10 to 15 minutes.

Let cool for 10 to 12 minutes – a little longer if you've cut the peel into very chunky pieces – then stir gently to disperse any scum. Pour into warm, sterilized jars and seal immediately (see pp. 21–22). Use within 2 years.

Variations

You can use both methods for making many other delicious marmalades:

Lemon marmalade with honey Use 2^1/$_4$ pounds of lemons instead of oranges, and omit the extra lemon juice. Replace 1^1/$_4$ cups of the sugar with ^{3}/$_4$ cup of honey, adding it at the same time.

Three-fruit marmalade Use a mixture of grapefruit, lemons, and sweet oranges to make a total of 2^1/$_4$ pounds of fruit.

Ruby red marmalade Both pink grapefruit and blood oranges make wonderful marmalades, though I prefer to use the sliced fruit method for these fruits. Add 3 tablespoons of lemon juice to every pound of fruit.

Seville and ginger marmalade Replace 1¹/₄ cups of the sugar with 9 ounces of chopped crystallized ginger, adding it along with the sugar.

Whiskey marmalade Add ¹/₄ cup of whiskey to the marmalade at the end of cooking.

P.S. Don't limit marmalade to the breakfast table, for its traits and qualities can be well used in other culinary ways. I like to replace candied peel in fruitcakes with a tablespoonful or two of marmalade, and I always add some to my Christmas mincemeat (p. 74). Marmalade makes a marvelous glaze for oven-baked ham, as well as sweet-and-sour chicken or pork dishes. Best of all, 3 or 4 tablespoonfuls will make a glorious golden topping for a good old-fashioned steamed pudding.

P.P.S. For generations, marmalade makers have cooked up the mass of seeds found inside citrus fruits in the belief that they are full of pectin. However, most of the pectin is actually found in the citrus peel, and I rely purely on this for the setting power in my marmalades.

Early rhubarb jam

Season: mid-January to late March

Early or forced rhubarb has been produced in West Yorkshire since the 1870s, as growers discovered that the heavy clay soil and cold winter climate suited the plant (a native of Siberia). Sequestered in dark sheds, carefully cultivated rhubarb crowns send forth slender, bright pink stems much more delicate in flavor than the thick green shafts of outdoor-grown rhubarb that appear later in the year.

This is one of my favorite ways to capture the earthy flavor of rhubarb. It's a plant that contains very little pectin, so the jam definitely requires an extra dose. The shortish boil time helps to preserve the fabulous color of the stems. I like to add a little Seville orange juice, but juice from sweet oranges works well too.

This light, soft jam is good mixed with yogurt or spooned over ice cream, or you can warm it and use to glaze a bread and butter pudding after baking.

Makes six 8-ounce jars

2^1/$_4$ pounds early rhubarb (untrimmed weight)

4^1/$_2$ cups granulated sugar blended with 2 teaspoons pectin powder

7 tablespoons freshly squeezed Seville or sweet orange juice

Wipe and trim the rhubarb and cut into ^{3}/$_4$- to 1-inch chunks. Pour a layer of sugar into the bottom of a preserving pan, then add a layer of rhubarb. Repeat, continuing until all the sugar and rhubarb are used, finishing with a layer of sugar. Pour the orange juice over the top. Cover and let stand for at least an hour or two – preferably overnight. This draws the juice from the rhubarb, and the resulting syrup helps keep the rhubarb chunks whole when boiled.

Gently bring the mixture to a boil, stirring carefully without crushing the rhubarb pieces. Boil rapidly for 5 to 6 minutes, then test for the setting point (see p. 41).

Remove from the heat and let rest for 5 minutes before pouring into warm, sterilized jars (see p. 21). Seal immediately (see p. 22). Use within 1 year.

Variations

Add 4 ounces of chopped crystallized ginger to the rhubarb, omitting the orange juice. Sharper-tasting main-crop rhubarb can also be used for this recipe – try adding a few young angelica leaves or a handful of fragrant rose petals.

Green gooseberry jam
with elderflower

Season: late May to June

I welcome the first tiny gooseberries that appear in the month of May, just as the first boughs of elderflowers are beginning to show. The berries are picked when small, almost as a thinning process, allowing their brothers and sisters to fill out and mature on the bush. But these early green goddesses are full of pectin, sharp, and tart, and make a divine jam. The fragrant elderflowers add a flavor that will remind you, when the days are short and dark, that summer will come again.

Makes six to seven 8-ounce jars
2¹/₄ pounds young gooseberries
About 8 heads of elderflower
5 cups granulated sugar

Top and tail the gooseberries (it's easiest to do this with a pair of scissors) and put into a preserving pan with 2 cups of water. Check the elderflower heads for any insects, then place on top of the gooseberries. Cook gently until the berries are soft but still hold their shape. Remove the elderflowers.

Add the sugar. Stir carefully, so as not to break up the fruit, until the sugar has dissolved, then bring to a full rolling boil and boil for 9 to 10 minutes. Test for the setting point (see p. 41).

Remove from the heat, let rest for 10 minutes, then pot and seal (see pp. 21–22). Use within 1 year.

Variation
Use this recipe for later-season gooseberries, without the elderflower. The fruit will be sweeter and the jam will have a soft pink color.

P.S. To make a quick and easy piquant gooseberry sauce to go with mackerel, add a little cider or balsamic vinegar to warmed gooseberry jam (with or without elderflower). Let the flavors mix and mingle before spooning over broiled or grilled fish.

Strawberry jam

Season: May to August

After a dismal result with my strawberry jam at the 2007 Uplyme and Lyme Regis Horticultural Show, I decided to get my act together and work out a recipe that I could rely on to get me that much-coveted first prize next time. My kitchen soon took on the appearance of a strawberry jam factory, with coded batches piled just about everywhere. I thought I'd nearly made the grade on batch three, but the tweaking for batch four caused mayhem in the jam pan. However, batch five seemed to come alive from the moment the lemon juice was added, and I knew it was going to be just right – bright in color, with some soft whole fruit and, of course, that wonderful, intense strawberry taste.

Strawberries are low in pectin. Using sugar with added pectin helps to attain a lovely set and a flavor that isn't too sickly sweet. Use freshly picked, dry fruit – not too big, or they'll blow to bits when the jam is bubbling away. However, if you're using very small fruit, make sure they're not too hard and seedy.

Makes five to six 8-ounce jars

2^1/$_4$ pounds strawberries, hulled, large ones halved or quartered

2^1/$_2$ cups granulated sugar

2^1/$_4$ cups granulated sugar blended with 1 teaspoon pectin powder

^{2}/$_3$ cup lemon juice

Put 7 ounces of the strawberries into a preserving pan with 1 cup of the plain granulated sugar. Crush to a pulp with a potato masher. Place the pan over gentle heat and, when the fruit mixture is warm, add the rest of the strawberries. Bring to a very gentle simmer, agitating the bottom of the pan with a wooden spoon to prevent the fruit from sticking. Simmer for 5 minutes to allow the strawberries to soften just a little.

Add the remaining 1^1/$_2$ cups plain granulated sugar and the sugar/pectin mixture. Stir gently to prevent the sugar from sticking and burning on the bottom of the pan. When the sugar has dissolved, add the lemon juice. Increase the heat and, when the mixture reaches a full boil, boil rapidly for 8 to 9 minutes. Then test for the setting point (see p. 41).

Remove from the heat and, if the surface is scummy, stir gently until the scum has dispersed. Pot and seal (see pp. 21–22). Use within 1 year.

Red currant jelly

Season: June to mid-July

Red currants make a superb and very versatile jelly. The red currant season is short, just a few weeks in midsummer, so make sure you don't miss it. If you haven't time to make your jelly straight away, you can pick the currants and freeze for later.

This is an endlessly useful jelly. A classic condiment to accompany roast lamb or game, it can also be used to enhance the flavor of gravies, casseroles, and piquant sauces. It makes an excellent glaze for fresh fruit tarts too.

Makes three to four 8-ounce jars
2¹/₄ pounds red currants
Granulated sugar

You don't have to top and tail the currants, or even take them off their stems. Simply wash them, put into a preserving pan with 1³/₄ cups of water, then simmer until they are very soft and have released all their juice. This will take about 45 minutes. Strain through a jelly strainer bag or cheesecloth (see p. 33) for several hours or overnight. Do not poke, squeeze, or force the pulp through the bag or you'll get cloudy jelly.

Measure the juice, put it into the cleaned preserving pan, and bring to a boil. For every cup of juice add 1 cup of sugar, adding it only when the juice is boiling. Stir until the sugar has dissolved, ensuring the sides of the pan are free of undissolved sugar crystals. Then boil rapidly for about 8 minutes, or until the setting point is reached (see p. 41).

Remove from the heat and stir to disperse any scum, then pour into warm, sterilized jars and seal (see pp. 21–22). Tap the jars to disperse any air bubbles caught in the jelly. Use within 1 year.

Variation
Add a couple of tablespoonfuls of chopped fresh mint to the jelly for the last 2 to 3 minutes of boiling.

P.S. Red currant jelly is the core ingredient of Cumberland sauce, a traditional partner to baked ham and game. Just add ¹/₄ cup of port, the grated zest of 1 orange and 1 unwaxed lemon, 1 teaspoon cayenne pepper, a pinch or two of English mustard powder (see p. 202), and perhaps a pinch of ground ginger to 10 tablespoons of red currant jelly.

Mum's black currant jam

Season: June to August

In my jam company days, when we would produce nearly fifteen thousand jars of preserves each week, my mum would still bring me jars of her homemade black currant jam. Sometimes I wondered if I needed another jar in the house, but I always enjoyed it immensely – black currant jam is an all-time favorite, with a flavor that is rarely rivaled. It's also very easy to make. The key is to ensure that the black currants are softened sufficiently before the sugar is added, or the skins will toughen and be unpleasantly chewy.

Use this in all the usual jammy ways with bread, toast, pancakes, yogurt, rice pudding, cakes, tarts, and, of course, scones and clotted cream.

Makes eight to ten 8-ounce jars
2¹/₄ pounds black currants
5 cups unrefined sugar

Pick over the black currants, removing any stems, twiggy bits, or damaged fruit (the dry, shriveled bit at one end is the remains of the flower and need not be removed).

Put the currants into a preserving pan with 2¹/₂ cups of water. Place over low heat and slowly bring to a simmer. Simmer for 15 to 20 minutes, until the fruit is soft but not disintegrated into a pulp.

Add the sugar and stir until it has dissolved. Then bring quickly to a full rolling boil. Boil hard for 5 minutes. Remove from the heat and continue to stir gently for a couple of minutes to reduce the temperature. Test for the setting point (see p. 41).

Let the jam cool a little and make sure the currants aren't bobbing above the surface when you pour it into warm, sterilized jam jars before sealing (see pp. 21–22). If they are, let the jam cool a little longer, and if they really won't submerge, then bring the jam back to a boil and boil for a couple minutes more. Use within 1 year.

P.S. The bittersweet leaves of the black currant bush can be used as a substitute for tea. Simply infuse the leaves in boiling water, steep for 10 minutes, then serve sweetened with a little honey.

Hugh's prizewinning
raspberry fridge jam

Season: June to October

Hugh Fearnley-Whittingstall, whose recipe this is, thinks the secret of success is to pick the raspberries on a hot, dry day, aiming for a good mixture of ripe and almost-ripe fruit, then to make the jam immediately to capture the full flavor of the berries.

The light boiling and lower-than-normal quantity of sugar produce a loose, soft-set jam with a fresh, tangy flavor. Low-sugar jams of this type are often called fridge jams (see p. 36). In fact, as long as it is capped when still above 195°F, this preserve will keep well in the pantry. However, once it is opened, you must keep it in the fridge. It won't last long after opening – maybe 2 or 3 weeks – but as it tastes so very, very good, this is unlikely to be a problem. It's one of those things you'll find yourself eating straight from the jar, maybe in the middle of the night!

This light, soft jam is fantastic in cakes or sherry trifles or stirred into creamy rice puddings. Best of all, layer it with toasted rolled oats, cream, Drambuie, and honey for a take on Cranachan, the traditional Scottish dessert.

Makes seven 8-ounce jars
3 pounds, 6 ounces raspberries

$3^3/_4$ **cups granulated sugar blended with $1^1/_2$ teaspoons pectin powder**

Start by picking over the raspberries very carefully and discarding any leaves or stems. Put half of the fruit into a preserving pan and use a potato masher to coarsely crush it. Add the remaining fruit and sugar (the mixture will look mouthwateringly good).

Stir over low heat to dissolve the sugar. Bring to a rolling boil, then boil for exactly 5 minutes. (If you prefer a firmer jam, continue boiling at this stage for a further 2 to 3 minutes.) Remove from the heat, stirring to disperse any scum.

It is important to pour and cap this low-sugar jam quickly (see pp. 21–22), but you must allow it to cool just a little first (give it 5 to 6 minutes) to prevent all those little raspberry seeds from rushing to the top of the jar, leaving you with half a jar of raspberry jelly and half a jar of raspberry seeds. Use within 1 year.

Variation
Flavorful ripe strawberries give very good results with this simple recipe too. Hull the strawberries, halve or quarter larger ones, and continue as above.

Plum jam

Season: August to September

Plums make a lovely jam and are rich in pectin and easy to prepare, so this is a great recipe for beginners. Just make sure the plums are tender and their skins well softened before adding the sugar. If not, the sugar hardens the skins and they'll be tough in the finished jam; they will also float to the top of the jar.

Makes ten 8-ounce jars
3 pounds, 6 ounces plums (see p. 202)
6$^1/_4$ cups granulated sugar

Halve and pit the plums. Crack open a few of the pits using a nutcracker and extract the kernels. Put these into a bowl and cover with boiling water. Let stand for a minute or so, then drain them and rub off the reddish brown skins. The kernels will add a lovely almondlike flavor to the jam.

Put the plums, skinned kernels, and 1$^3/_4$ cups of water into a preserving pan. Bring to a simmer and cook gently until the fruit is tender and the skins soft – this should take about 20 minutes but depends on the variety and size of plum.

Add the sugar and stir until dissolved. Bring to a boil and boil rapidly until the setting point is reached (see p. 41), usually 10 to 12 minutes. Remove from the heat. If the fruit is bobbing about at the surface, it's probably not cooked well enough (the sugar is heavier than the plums, and the jam must cook sufficiently for the fruit to absorb the sugar). If this happens, boil for a further 2 to 4 minutes.

Pot the jam and seal (see pp. 21–22). Use within 1 year.

Variations

Replace some of the water with freshly squeezed orange juice and/or add 2 cinnamon sticks. Another nice twist is to add $^3/_4$ cup of chopped walnuts to the jam toward the end of the boiling time.

Apple, herb, and flower jellies

Season: late summer to autumn

The aromatic essences of fresh herbs and flowers can be captured beautifully in a jelly. These preserves are great to have in the kitchen, as they add a sweet piquancy to all kinds of food, simple and rich. Cooking apples and crab apples are both ideal choices for the basic jelly. Excellent sources of pectin and acid, they nevertheless have gentle flavors that will not overwhelm the herbs.

Serve mint jelly with lamb, sage with fish, basil with poultry or game, parsley with ham, and rose-petal jelly (see below) with wafer-thin, buttered bread. Any herb jelly will also be delicious with soft cheeses, pâtés, and terrines.

Makes four to five 8-ounce jars

3 pounds, 6 ounces cooking apples
1 medium bunch of sage, rosemary, mint, tarragon, thyme, or basil

7 tablespoons cider vinegar
Granulated sugar

Coarsely chop the apples, discarding any bad parts, but don't peel or core them. Place in a preserving pan with the herbs, reserving half a dozen small sprigs to put into the jars. Barely cover the apples with water. Bring to a boil, then simmer gently, covered, for 45 minutes to 1 hour, until the fruit is very soft. Pour the contents of the pan into a jelly strainer bag or piece of cheesecloth suspended over a bowl (see p. 33) and leave to drip for at least 2 hours, or overnight.

Measure the strained juice. For every cup of juice, measure out 1 cup of sugar. Return the juice to the cleaned-out pan and add the vinegar. Heat to a boil, then add the sugar and stir until dissolved. Increase the heat and boil rapidly for 10 to 12 minutes, until the setting point is reached (see p. 41). Remove from the heat and skim with a slotted spoon to remove any scum.

Pour into small, warm, sterilized jars (see p. 21), adding an herb sprig to each. Cover and seal (see p. 22). Use within 1 year.

Variations

For stronger-flavored jellies, you can add 3 to 4 tablespoons of freshly chopped herbs after removing the jelly from the heat. Allow to cool for 10 minutes before potting. For exquisite rose-petal or dandelion jelly, add 1 ounce of scented petals instead of herbs. The above method can also be used to make quince jelly, replacing the apples with quince and leaving out the herbs.

Blackberry and apple leather

Season: late August to September

Fruit leathers are thin, pliable sheets of dried, sweetened fruit purée with a flexible consistency like leather. To be truthful, I had always avoided making them, thinking they sounded complicated. But in a spirit of experimentation, I decided to try some out. They were a revelation. I discovered how easy it is to create these strong, semitransparent sheets, and how versatile they are. They are fun to use and eat – you can cut them, roll them, fold them, and pack them away. Light and easy to carry, they're full of fruity energy, so they're great for lunch boxes or long walks. Snip off pieces to dissolve gently into fruit salads, or save them for the festive season when their translucent, jewel-like colors will look gorgeous on the Christmas tree.

Makes two 10 by 12-inch sheets
1 pound, 2 ounces blackberries
1 pound, 2 ounces peeled, cored,
    and chopped cooking apples
    (2–3 large apples)

Juice of 1 lemon
7 tablespoons honey

Preheat the oven to a very low setting – I use 140°F (approximately). Line two baking sheets, measuring about 10 by 12 inches, with parchment paper.

Put the blackberries, apples, and lemon juice into a pan. Cook gently until soft and pulpy, about 20 minutes. Press the mixture through a sieve or food mill into a bowl; you should have about 1¹/₂ pounds of fruit purée. Add the honey and mix well.

Divide the purée between the two baking sheets. Spread it out lightly with the back of a spoon until the purée covers each sheet in a thin, even layer.

Put the baking sheets in the oven for 12 to 18 hours, until the fruit purée is completely dry and easily peels off the parchment. Roll up the leather in parchment or waxed paper and store in an airtight container. Use within 5 months.

Variations
There is no end to the possible variations here – you can turn any fruit into a leather. All you need to do is create a smooth, thick purée with your chosen fruit before drying it out. Try plums, spicing the purée with a little cinnamon; or peaches, infusing them with a few honeysuckle blossoms as they cook. For a savory leather, use half apples and half tomatoes seasoned with 2 teaspoons of souper mix (p. 199) or celery salt.

Apple lemon curd

Season: late August to January

When I made preserves for a living, I tried all kinds of curds, from orange to passion fruit, but none of them was ever quite as popular as the good old-fashioned lemon variety. I didn't think I could improve on it until recently, when I came across an old recipe for an apple-y lemon curd. I tried it out, and I now prefer it even to a classic straight lemon curd – it's like eating apples and custard: softly sweet, tangy, and quite, quite delicious.

Makes four 8-ounce jars

1 pound Granny Smith apples, peeled, cored, and chopped

Finely grated zest and juice of 2 unwaxed lemons (you need 7 tablespoons strained juice)

$1/2$ cup plus 1 tablespoon unsalted butter

$2^1/4$ cups granulated sugar

$3/4$ cup plus 2 tablespoons beaten eggs (4 or 5 large eggs)

Put the chopped apples into a pan with 7 tablespoons of water and the lemon zest. Cook gently until soft and fluffy, then either beat to a purée with a wooden spoon or run through a food mill.

Put the lemon juice, butter, sugar, and apple purée into a double boiler or heatproof bowl over a pan of simmering water. As soon as the butter has melted and the mixture is hot and glossy, pour in the eggs through a sieve, then whisk with a balloon whisk. If the fruit purée is too hot when the beaten egg is added, the egg will curdle. One way to guard against this is to check the temperature of the purée with a candy thermometer – it should be no higher than 130° to 140°F when the egg is added. If your curd does curdle, take the pan off the heat and whisk vigorously until smooth.

Stir the mixture over low heat, scraping down the sides of the bowl every few minutes, until thick and creamy. This will take 9 to 10 minutes; the temperature should reach 180° to 183°F on a candy thermometer. Immediately pour into warm, sterilized jars and seal (see pp. 21–22). Use within 1 month. Once opened, keep in the fridge.

Variations

To make gooseberry curd, replace the apples with gooseberries. If you'd like a traditional, pure lemon curd, leave out the apples, increase the lemon juice to $3/4$ cup plus 2 tablespoons (4 to 5 lemons) and add the grated zest of 2 or 3 more lemons.

Hedgerow jelly

Season: September to October

The months of September and October allow us to reap the berried treasure of the hedgerows – a seasonal activity that is not without its dangers, as many wild fruits are guarded by all sorts of thorns, prickles, and entangling stems. However, with a little common sense and determination you should be able to overcome these country hurdles, and the basketful of fruit you bring home will be a just reward.

At the heart of all the best hedgerow jellies is the crab apple (*Malus* species). The pectin in this often scarred and scabby pomaceous fruit lends the setting power that many hedgerow berries lack. Crab apples produce a stunning pink jelly when used on their own, too.

For this recipe, you can use crab apples, rosehips, hawthorn berries, blackberries, elderberries, or rowanberries (mountain ash berries). Usually, I go for about 50 percent crab apples with a combination of two or three different berries. If I've gathered rosehips or rowanberries, however, I prefer to use them on their own, blended only with crab apple (see the variations on p. 70).

Makes about six 8-ounce jars
2^1/4 pounds crab apples (or cooking apples)
2^1/4 pounds mixed hedgerow berries (see above)
About 5 cups granulated sugar

Pick over your fruit, removing the stems and leafy bits and rinsing the berries if necessary. Don't peel or core the apples (the peel and core are excellent sources of pectin); just chop them coarsely. Place all of the prepared fruit in a saucepan with 5 cups of water. Bring gently to a simmer, and simmer until the fruit is soft and pulpy. Remove from the heat.

Have ready a jelly strainer bag or piece of cheesecloth (see p. 33) and turn the contents of the pan into it. Leave to drip overnight. The jelly will turn cloudy if you squeeze the juice through, so just let it drip at its own pace.

The next day, measure the juice – you will probably have about 5 cups, though this will depend on the berries used. For every cup of juice, allow 1 cup of sugar. Put the juice into a large pan and bring slowly to a boil. Add the sugar as it just comes to a boil and keep stirring until the sugar has dissolved. Then boil rapidly, without

(continued)

stirring, for 9 to 10 minutes until the setting point is reached (see p. 41). Skim the jelly and pot and seal as quickly as possible (see pp. 21–22). Use within 1 year.

Variations

These are some of my favorite takes on the hedgerow jelly idea. In each case, follow the hedgerow jelly method and quantities on p. 69; i.e., always use 1 cup of sugar for each cup of strained fruit juice.

Spicy crab apple jelly Use crab apples alone and add a few cloves and a couple of cinnamon sticks when the fruit is being cooked. This all-time classic hedgerow jelly is equally at home on thinly sliced hot buttered toast or as an accompaniment to succulent cold roast pork or turkey.

Rosehip and apple jelly Use 1 pound, 2 ounces of rosehips, first chopped in a food processor, and 3 pounds, 6 ounces of crab or cooking apples. Rosehips from the wild rose or dog rose seem to have a better flavor than those from cultivated roses. However, some garden varieties of rose also produce cookable hips – notably *Rosa rugosa*. If you want to harvest rosehips from your garden, do not deadhead your roses. Excellent with roast pork.

Rowan jelly Use 2¼ pounds of rowanberries (mountain ash berries) and 2¼ pounds of crab apples. Add the juice of 1 lemon before adding the sugar. For a really aromatic jelly, add a bunch of sage or thyme when the fruit is softening. Rowan jelly is lovely served with game.

Blackberry and apple jelly Use 2¼ pounds of blackberries and 2¼ pounds of apples. This is a nostalgic teatime treat for me, as I remember how good my grandmother's blackberry and apple jelly always tasted on wafer-thin slices of buttered bread.

P.S. Hedgerow jelly, or any other well-colored jelly, can be used as a natural coloring for glacé icing. Just a teaspoonful or two will be sufficient to give your icing a wickedly deep hue that will be sure to liven up your cakes.

Honeyed hazels

Season: September

You've got to be quick to beat the squirrels to the hazelnuts each autumn. Once you have found some, it's important to store them carefully. Even with their shells on, they have a tendency to dry out and shrivel up, but preserving them in honey will keep them fresh and fragrant for ages. Use wild hazels that you have gathered yourself, or filberts, which are simply a cultivated form of hazelnut.

Spoon your honeyed hazels over plain yogurt, chocolate ice cream, porridge, or muesli.

Makes about three 4-ounce jars
1 pound, 2 ounces hazelnuts or filberts
1 cup pale honey

Start by inviting your friends round for a nut-cracking evening (they'll come the first year, but maybe not the next). Crack all the nuts and remove the kernels.

Heat a frying pan over low heat. Toast the shelled nuts in batches for 4 to 5 minutes, jiggling and shaking the pan to make sure they don't burn. Remove from the heat and allow to cool.

Pack the nuts into sterilized jars (see p. 21), adding 1 tablespoon of the honey at every third or fourth layer. Continue until the jars are chock-a-block full, making sure that the nuts are well covered in honey. Seal securely with a lid (see p. 22) and store in a cool, dry, dark place. Use within 1 year.

P.S. Pale honey is runny, while dark honey is thick and opaque, but apart from this there is no real difference between the two types – it's just down to the feeding ground for the bees. Borage honey, a speciality of east Yorkshire, is one of the clearest honeys you will ever come across, whereas clover honey is favored for its creamy, thick texture and floral flavor. All honey, with the exception of heather honey, will eventually become cloudy as a result of the natural process of crystallization. If you find this happens and you want your honey to be runny again, then just stand the jar in a bowl of hot water for a few minutes until it is liquid honey again.

Plum and apple mincemeat

Season: September to October

The term *mincemeat* originated in the fifteenth century, when chopped meat was preserved with a combination of dried fruit, sugar, and aromatic spices. During the seventeenth century, suet replaced the meat and has been used ever since. This recipe is a departure on several fronts: it uses fresh fruit as well as dried, and it contains no suet. In fact, it contains very little fat (only the oil in the walnuts). The result is light and fruity, but with all the rich, warm spiciness of a traditional mincemeat. If you can't find russet apples, any good eating apple can be used.

Makes four 12-ounce jars

2^1/$_4$ pounds plums

Finely grated zest and juice of 2 to 3 oranges (you need ^{3}/$_4$ cup plus 2 tablespoons juice)

1 pound, 2 ounces russet apples, peeled, cored, and chopped into ^{3}/$_8$-inch cubes

1^1/$_4$ cups currants

1^1/$_4$ cups raisins

1^1/$_4$ cups golden raisins

^{1}/$_3$ cup orange marmalade

1^1/$_4$ cups Demerara sugar

½ teaspoon ground cloves

2 teaspoons ground ginger

½ of a whole nutmeg, grated

^{1}/$_4$ cup ginger wine or cordial (optional)

^{3}/$_4$ cup chopped walnuts

^{1}/$_4$ cup brandy or sloe gin

Wash the plums, halve and pit them, then put them into a saucepan with the orange juice. Cook gently until tender, about 15 minutes. Purée in a blender or press through a sieve. You should end up with about 3 cups of plum purée.

Put the purée into a large bowl and add all the other ingredients, except the brandy or gin. Mix thoroughly, then cover and let stand for 12 hours.

Preheat the oven to 250°F. Put the mincemeat in a large baking dish and bake, uncovered, for 2 to 2½ hours. Stir in the brandy or gin, then spoon into warm, sterilized jars (see p. 21), making sure there aren't any air pockets. Seal (see p. 22) and store in a dry, dark, cool place until Christmas. Use within 1 year.

Variations

You can vary this recipe, but keep the fresh fruit purée to around 3 cups and the total amount of dried fruit to 4 cups or 1^1/$_4$ pounds. For an apple, pear, and ginger mincemeat, replace the plums with Granny Smith apples, the russet apples with firm pears, and $^2/_3$ cup of either of the raisins with $3^1/_2$ ounces of crystallized ginger. You could also exchange the walnuts for almonds and add a couple of teaspoonfuls of ground cinnamon.

Quince cheese

Season: late September to October

A fruit cheese is simply a solid, sliceable preserve – and the princely quince, with its exquisite scent and delicately grainy texture, makes the most majestic one of all. It can be potted in small molds to turn out, slice, and eat with cheese. Alternatively, you can pour it into shallow trays to set, then cut it into cubes, coat with sugar, and serve as a sweetmeat.

A little coarsely chopped quince cheese adds a delicious fruity note to lamb stews or tagines – or try combining it with chopped apple for a pie or crumble.

Makes about 2¼ pounds
2¼ pounds quince
2½ to 3¾ cups granulated sugar

Food-grade paraffin wax, for sealing

Wash the quince. Coarsely chop the fruit but don't peel or core it. Place in a large pan and barely cover with water. Bring to a simmer and cook until soft and pulpy, adding a little more water if necessary. Let stand for several hours.

Press the contents of the pan through a sieve or run through a food mill. Weigh the pulp and return it to the cleaned-out pan, adding an equal weight of sugar. Bring gently to a boil, stirring until the sugar has dissolved, then simmer gently, stirring frequently, for an hour and a bit until really thick and glossy. It may bubble and spit like a volcano, so do take care. The mixture is ready when it is so thick that you can scrape a spoon through it and see the bottom of the pan for a couple of seconds before the mixture oozes together again.

If you're using small dishes or straight-sided jars, brush them with a little glycerine. This will make it easy to turn out the cheese. If you're using a shallow baking pan or something similar, line it with parchment or waxed paper, allowing plenty of overhang to wrap the finished cheese.

When the cheese is cooked, pour it into the prepared molds or jars. To seal open molds, pour melted food-grade paraffin wax over the hot fruit cheese. Jars can be sealed with lids (see pp. 21–22). Cheese set in a shallow tray should be covered with parchment or waxed paper and kept in the fridge.

For optimum flavor, allow the quince cheese to mature for 4 to 6 weeks. Use within 1 year.

Melissa's chestnut jam

Season: October to December

I first made this deliciously sweet preserve while staying at a farm on Dartmoor. Melissa, who lived at the farm, came to help with the laborious job of peeling the chestnuts, and we whipped through them in no time. Adding honey to the jam seemed entirely appropriate, since that's what Melissa means in Greek.

I like to spoon chestnut jam into meringue nests and top with cream. Or stir a spoonful or two into chocolate mousse, or dollop it on vanilla ice cream before drizzling with hot chocolate sauce. This preserve also makes a lovely filling for chocolate cakes, and, of course, it can be enjoyed simply spread on crusty bread.

Makes four 8-ounce jars

2$^1/_4$ pounds sweet chestnuts
2 cups granulated sugar
1 teaspoon vanilla paste or extract
$^1/_4$ cup honey
$^1/_4$ cup brandy

The first task is to remove the leathery shells and skins from the chestnuts. Use a sharp knife to make a nick in the top of each chestnut. Plunge them into a pan of boiling water for 2 to 3 minutes – sufficient time to soften the shell but not let the nuts get piping hot and difficult to handle. Remove the pan from the heat. Fish out half a dozen or so chestnuts and peel off their coats. With luck, the thin brown skin under the shell will peel away too. Continue in this way until all are peeled.

Put the chestnuts into a clean pan and add water to just cover the chestnuts. Bring to a boil and simmer for 25 to 30 minutes, until tender. Drain, but keep the cooking liquid.

Purée the chestnuts with $^1/_2$ cup of the cooking liquid in a food processor or using a handheld blender.

Pour a further 6 tablespoons of the cooking liquid into a pan and add the sugar. Heat gently until dissolved. Add the chestnut purée, vanilla paste or extract, and honey. Stir until well blended. Bring to a boil, then cook gently for 5 to 10 minutes, until well thickened. Take care, as it will pop and splutter and may spit. Remove from the heat and stir in the brandy. Pour into warm, sterilized jars and seal immediately (see pp. 21–22). Use within 6 months. Store in the fridge once opened.

Candied orange sticks

Season: anytime

I like to make several batches of these sweets in November or early December. A dozen or so, wrapped in cellophane, are a charming gift. Needless to say, you don't need to stop at oranges: lemon and grapefruit peel work equally well, and you can use milk chocolate, dark chocolate, or white chocolate for dipping. The corn syrup is optional, but does prevent the sticks from becoming too hard. It is best to keep the candied sticks in an airtight container and only dip them in chocolate shortly before you want them.

Makes about 100 sticks

4 or 5 large oranges
$2^1/_2$ cups granulated sugar

1 tablespoon corn syrup (optional)
7 ounces good dark chocolate

Scrub the oranges, then remove the peel in quarters. To do this, cut through the peel with a sharp knife, going right around the orange, starting and finishing at the stem end, then repeat at a right angle to the first cut. Remove the peel, with the attached pith, from the fruit. Weigh out 9 ounces of peel and cut it into slices measuring about $^1/_4$ by 2 inches.

Put the orange peel slices into a large pan and cover with 8 cups of cold water. Bring to a boil and simmer for 5 minutes. Drain and return to the pan with 4 cups of cold water. Bring to a boil and simmer, covered, for 45 minutes. Add the sugar and stir until dissolved (it won't take long). Simmer, covered, for 30 minutes. Remove from the heat and let stand for 24 hours.

Bring the pan to a boil again. Add the corn syrup, if using, and boil gently, uncovered, for 30 minutes, or until all the liquid has evaporated and the orange sticks are coated with bubbling orange syrup. Remove from the heat and allow to cool. Using a pair of tongs (or your fingers), carefully remove the orange sticks and place on a wire rack with a tray underneath to catch the drips. Leave in a warm place for 24 hours, or place in a very low oven at approximately 140°F for 2 to 3 hours to dry.

Break the chocolate into pieces, put into a heatproof bowl over a pan of simmering water, and leave until melted. Remove from the heat. Dip one half of each orange stick in the melted chocolate and place on a sheet of parchment or waxed paper to dry.

Before dipping, the sticks will keep well for 3 to 4 months. Once they have their chocolate coating, they are best eaten within 3 weeks.

Cider apple butter

Autumn is the season for apples. For centuries, the apple crop has been important, and the apple tree cherished and celebrated for its fruit. Wassailing is an English West Country tradition when, on Twelfth Night of old (January 17), country folk toast and drink to the health of the largest and most prolific apple tree in the orchard for a healthy, fruitful crop the coming season.

The sharp and bittersweet qualities of cider give this old-fashioned apple butter a special flavor. It's a sensational fruity spread to daub over hot buttered toast or crumpets.

Makes four to five 8-ounce jars
3 pounds, 6 ounces cooking apples
2¹/₂ cups dry or medium cider
Granulated sugar

½ teaspoon ground cloves
½ teaspoon ground cinnamon

There is no need to peel or core the apples. However, if you are using windfalls (and this is a very good recipe in which to do so), cut away any damaged or bruised bits. Chop the apples into fairly big pieces (each into about 8). Place in a large pan with the cider and 2¹/₂ cups of water. Cook gently until soft, then remove from the heat.

Push the apple mixture through a sieve or use a food mill to reduce it to a purée. Measure the volume of fruit pulp and return it to the cleaned-out pan, adding ²/₃ cup of sugar for every cup of fruit pulp. Add the cloves and cinnamon. Slowly bring to a boil, stirring until the sugar has dissolved, then boil rapidly for 10 to 15 minutes, until the mixture begins to splutter and is thick and creamy.

Remove from the heat and pour immediately into warm, sterilized jars (it's best to use small jars, as this low-sugar preserve has a relatively short shelf life once opened), then seal immediately (see pp. 21–22). Use within 1 year. Store in the fridge once opened.

Variation
Blackberries make a beautiful fruit butter. Follow the above method using 2¹/₄ pounds of ripe blackberries, 1 pound, 2 ounces of cored and peeled cooking apples, and 7 tablespoons of lemon juice; use ¹/₂ cup plus 1 tablespoon of sugar for every cup of fruit pulp.

Compost heap jelly

Season: anytime

This is a wonderful, frugal recipe that complements some of the other fruity preserves in the book because it uses the apple scraps and citrus skins that would normally be destined for the compost heap or bin. These skins are full of flavor and rich in pectin, so it's a shame not to use them. For the cost of a bag of sugar (and a bit of your time), you can transform them into a really fruity, marmalade-flavored jelly. It functions nicely as an emergency breakfast preserve when your last jar of marmalade has been eaten and the seasonal Sevilles haven't yet arrived in the shops.

Makes about five 4-ounce jars

1 pound, 2 ounces apple cores and peel

1 pound, 2 ounces citrus fruit peel (unwaxed lemon, orange, grapefruit and/or lime), cut into about $^3/_8$-inch shreds

Granulated sugar

Juice of 1 orange, lemon, or grapefruit (optional)

Put the apple cores and peel and the citrus peel into a saucepan. Add sufficient water to cover (you'll probably need about 6 cups). Bring to a simmer and cook slowly for 45 to 60 minutes – this softens the fruit and releases the valuable pectin. Turn the fruit into a jelly strainer bag or piece of cheesecloth (see p. 33) and leave overnight to drip.

Measure the strained liquid and allow 1 cup of sugar for every cup of juice. Return the juice to the pan and add the orange, lemon, or grapefruit juice, if using. Bring to a boil, then add the sugar. Stir until dissolved, then boil rapidly, without stirring, until the setting point is reached (see p. 41), about 10 minutes or so.

Remove from the heat and stir, always going in the same direction, until all the surface bubbles have disappeared. Pour into warm, sterilized jars (see p. 21) and either swivel or tap the side of the jars to remove any remaining bubbles. Seal in the usual way (see p. 22). Use within 1 year.

Pickles, Chutneys & Relishes

Time for vinegar vapors

to fill the air! This chapter is a little sharper than the last one – and full of recipes that feature piquancy, bite, and spice. These sweet-sour preserves are generally inexpensive and easy to make. There are only a few guidelines to follow – you don't have to worry about pectin or acid, for instance, as in jam making. Their uses extend far beyond cold meat and ploughman's lunches. They can be stirred into soups; added to meaty stews, curries, or tagines; served with smoked or marinated fish; and, of course, combined with other ingredients to make great sandwiches and picnic food. No home should be without them! Often lumped together, pickles, chutneys, and relishes are actually distinctly different and not prepared in the same way.

Clear pickles These are an age-old way of preserving vegetables or fruits, which are usually left raw or only lightly cooked, and kept whole or in large pieces. Pickles rely predominantly on vinegar and salt for keepability, though sugar, honey, spices, and herbs can all be added for extra flavor. After salting (see p. 88), the ingredients are rinsed and drained before being packed into jars and fully covered with plain or spiced vinegar. Pickled onions are the classic example of this type of preserve.

Sweet pickles Made from fruits and vegetables, again in relatively large pieces, and lightly cooked in sweetened vinegar, these are often flavored with spices such as ginger, cloves, and allspice. In some recipes – piccalilli, for instance – the vinegar syrup is thickened with cornstarch to make a light sauce. The cooked produce is packed in warm jars and the vinegar syrup is reduced and poured over the fruit to cover.

Chutneys Authentic Indian chutneys are usually fresh preparations served with spicy foods. The Western interpretation of a chutney is rather different: rich, highly spiced, sweet-sharp preserves, based on vegetables and fruits that are chopped small and cooked for a long time to create a spoonable consistency and mellow flavor. They often feature dried fruit too, which contribute natural sugar and textural contrast.

Relishes Somewhere between pickles and chutneys, these are made from diced or chunkily cut fruit and vegetables, but they are cooked for a shorter time than a chutney. They can be spicy, sweet, or sour (or all three), may be eaten soon after making; and should be kept in the fridge once opened.

Essential ingredients

Pickles, chutneys, and relishes customarily rely on vinegar or a mix of vinegar, salt, and/or sugar to preserve tender, young vegetables and fruit. Highly flavored spices or herbs are added to augment the final flavor, but their often fiery potency will mellow as the preserve matures.

Salt

Salt plays a very important role in the making of pickles, chutneys, and relishes and, indeed, can be used as the sole preservative, as in preserved lemons (p. 118). However, it's more usually employed as a general flavor enhancer and in the preparation of vegetables and fruit prior to pickling. It may be sprinkled straight on the ingredients (this is known as dry-salting) or made into a brine (wet-salting), in which the ingredients are immersed and left for 12 to 24 hours. The salt firms up the vegetables and removes excess water which would otherwise dilute the vinegar and cause the pickles to turn moldy. Dry-salting is ideal for watery vegetables such as cucumbers and summer squash, and for very crisp pickles, whereas brine is less harsh and can be used for less juicy produce. A fine-grained salt is essential for dry-salting, as it will adhere closely to the surface of the ingredient, but any good-quality salt can be used in a brine. See p. 30 for more information on different types of salt.

> To make brine For a good all-purpose brine, allow 1 heaping tablespoon of salt per cup of water (a lighter brine is more appropriate for small ingredients such as nasturtium seeds). Simply dissolve the salt in the water and the brine is ready to use. The prepared ingredients should be covered with the brine and left overnight or for up to 24 hours before being drained, dried, packed, and pickled in jars. Many old recipes call for the brine to be "strong enough to float an egg"; you will find this ratio will do just that.

> To dry-salt Layer your cut-up vegetables on a shallow dish, sprinkling fine salt over each layer. As in brining, the vegetables are left overnight or for up to 24 hours. After a few hours, you will see water being drawn from the vegetables. After salting, the ingredients need to be rinsed in very cold water (to keep them crisp), drained well, and patted dry before being pickled.

Vinegar

Your pickles, chutneys, and relishes will only be as good as the vinegar you use. If vinegar is the main preserving ingredient, it's important to use a good-quality variety with at least 5 percent acetic acid content (you should find this information on the bottle). Beyond that, there are no hard-and-fast rules as to the type of vinegar you should go for – it's very much a matter of taste (see p. 29 for more information on different types). However, a translucent vinegar gives a better appearance in a clear pickle. The vinegar used for pickling is almost always spiced. You can buy ready-spiced pickling vinegars, commonly based on malt vinegar. However, I prefer to make my own at home, so I can choose the type of vinegar and the precise spice mix.

Spices

Spices are essential to give fiery bite, flavor, and aroma to pickles, chutneys, and relishes. Whole spices are used for pickles – ground ones produce a cloudy result – but either whole or freshly ground spices can be used for chutneys and relishes. Whole spices should be tied in a cheesecloth bag or enclosed in a tea or spice infuser so they can be easily removed after cooking.

To make a cheesecloth spice bag, cut a piece of cheesecloth, about 8 inches square, put the spices in a heap in the middle, and gather up the edges of the cheesecloth to form a little sack. Tie the bag with string so that the spices are loosely but securely held in.

A pickling spice blend can be bought ready-made but you'll get a much fresher flavor if you make your own – I combine equal quantities of cinnamon stick, whole cloves, mace blades, and whole allspice and a few peppercorns and allow $1/2$ to 1 ounce of this mix for every 4 cups of vinegar. I like to add a good tablespoonful of Demerara sugar and a couple of fresh bay leaves when I brew up the spice. The mix can be kept in an airtight jar for at least 1 year and used as required. Other spices such as fresh or dried chiles, and fennel, dill, or celery seeds can also be added to bring a different range of flavors to your pickles.

Always check the sell-by date on your spices and be ruthless about getting rid of any that are past their best. Once they reach a certain age, they'll lose the aroma and flavor you need. If you are using ground spice in a recipe, it is always worth taking the time to grind your own because, once ground, spices lose their pungency amazingly quickly. Give whole spices a light toasting in a dry frying pan, then grind as finely as possible in a mortar and pestle or a spice or coffee grinder. Prepare the spices in small quantities and don't keep the mix for more than a week or two.

Vegetables and fruits

Vegetables and fruits, which will make up the bulk and body of your preserves, should be young, firm, and as fresh as possible. Almost any produce can be used, though soft berries are generally better in jams and jellies. I've made pickles, chutneys, and relishes with just about everything else! Apples, gooseberries, pears, plums, summer squash, and tomatoes (ripe or green) form the base of most chutneys. For most recipes they should be peeled, washed, and well drained before being chopped, diced, or left whole. Cut away any bruised or damaged flesh.

Making perfect pickles

Pickles are very easy to make and their success relies quite simply on good preparation of the raw ingredients, a well-spiced vinegar, and an adequate maturing period.

1. After brining or salting your prepared fruit or vegetables, rinse and drain them well.

2. To prevent bruising, don't pack the produce too tightly into the jars.

3. Pack in an attractive way to within 1 inch of the top of the jar, leaving enough room for the contents to be completely covered with vinegar.

4. Always use sterilized jars (see p. 21) and vinegar-proof lids.

5. Use cold vinegar for crisp pickles and hot vinegar if a softer texture is required.

6. Store your pickles in a cool, dark, dry place for at least 1 month before using.

Making perfect chutneys

Don't rush your chutney making, for a good chutney will take several hours to make. The end result will be more than worthy of the time you've spent.

1. Use a stainless steel pan and wooden spoon – other materials may react with the vinegar and cause discoloration.

2. Cut fruit and vegetables into small, even-sized pieces – this is time-consuming but really crucial in achieving a good final texture.

3. Long, slow cooking in an open pan is essential for the chutney to become rich, smooth, and mellow.

4. Toward the end of cooking, stir frequently so the chutney doesn't stick to the bottom of the pan.

5. The chutney has reached the right consistency when you can draw a wooden spoon across the bottom of the pan and see a clear line for a few seconds before the chutney comes together again.

6. Fill jars to within $1/4$ inch of the top and cover with vinegar-proof lids. Poorly covered chutney will dry out and shrink in the jar.

7. Store chutneys in a cool, dark, dry place and let them mature for at least 8 weeks before using.

Spring rhubarb relish

Season: May to July

Made with the reddish green stalks of main-crop or field rhubarb, this relish is quick and easy, involving much less cooking than a chutney would require. It is light, very fruity, and not too sweet. Delicious with curries, oily fish, chicken, and cheese and in sandwiches, it's a versatile addition to the larder.

Rhubarb, by the way, is very easy to prepare, but do take care to always remove the leaves, as they are poisonous.

Makes five 8-ounce jars

For the spice bag
2 ounces fresh ginger, bruised
2 cinnamon sticks, snapped in half
6 cloves

$2^1/_2$ cups granulated sugar
7 tablespoons cider vinegar
$2^1/_4$ pounds rhubarb
(untrimmed weight)
$^3/_4$ cup raisins

First, make your spice bag by tying up the ginger, cinnamon sticks, and cloves in an 8-inch square of cheesecloth.

Put the sugar, vinegar, 7 tablespoons of water, and the spice bag into a preserving pan. Heat gently to dissolve the sugar and allow the spices to release their flavors into the syrup. Remove from the heat and set aside to infuse for about 20 minutes.

Meanwhile, trim and wipe the rhubarb stalks and chop into $^3/_4$- to 1-inch chunks.

Add the rhubarb and raisins to the spiced syrup. Cook gently for 15 to 20 minutes, until the mixture is thick but the rhubarb is still discernible as soft chunks. Remove from the heat; pour into warm, sterilized jars; and seal with vinegar-proof lids (see pp. 21–22). Use within 1 year.

P.S. To bruise the ginger for the spice bag, simply whack it gently with a rolling pin or similar blunt object.

Variation

Gooseberries will stand in quite readily for the rhubarb in this recipe. For the spice bag, try using a mix of traditional Indian spices: 1 teaspoon yellow mustard seeds and ½ teaspoon each of fennel, cumin, nigella, and fenugreek seeds.

Chile pepper jelly

Season: late summer to autumn

The beauty of this recipe is that it is so very simple. Moreover, you can turn up the heat or cool it down to suit your mood by the variety of the chile pepper you use. In the late summer and autumn, look for hot fruity habaneros, rich mild poblanos, tiny hot Thai chiles, or flaming jalapeños to use in this sizzling jelly relish. I like to use red bell peppers, as they are symbolic of the heat, but, of course, there's no reason why you can't use yellow, orange, or green, or a mixture of all four.

Use this punchy jelly with cream cheese, smoked mackerel, rice dishes, and crispy stir-fried vegetables.

Makes five 8-ounce jars
1 pound, 10 ounces red bell peppers
3¹/₂ ounces jalapeños or other chiles
2 ounces fresh ginger, peeled
1¹/₂ cups cider vinegar

5 cups granulated sugar blended with
   2 teaspoons pectin powder
¹/₄ cup freshly squeezed lime juice
   (1 to 2 limes)
1 teaspoon salt

Start by slicing both the bell peppers and the chiles in half lengthwise and removing the fibrous tissue and countless seeds. Make sure you wash your hands after handling chiles and avoid touching your eyes for awhile, as the chile oil will burn them. Finely chop the peppers, chiles, and ginger by hand or in a food processor. Place in a large pan, add the vinegar, and slowly bring to a simmer. Add the sugar mixture, lime juice, and salt, stirring until the sugar has dissolved and the mixture begins to boil.

Boil for 4 to 6 minutes, and then remove from the heat. Allow to cool for 5 minutes, then pour into clean, sterilized jars and seal with vinegar-proof lids (see pp. 21–22). Use within 1 year.

P.S. If you find the pepper pieces rise to the top of the jar as you pot the jelly, let the jars cool to room temperature, then give them a quick swirl – the pepper pieces will redistribute and remain well suspended in the cooling jelly.

Pickled garlic

Season: May to August

Garlic is the strongest-tasting member of the *Allium* family, and the moodiest too. It can change character considerably depending on how it is treated. Left whole and cooked slowly, it is gentle and soft. Chopped up, it will release a little more of its pungent aroma, while crushed to a paste it attains the strong, sometimes bitter flavor that makes it notorious.

When pickled, it remains crisp to the bite, but the flavor becomes really quite mellow – you can eat the cloves straight from the jar. I like to slice the pickled garlic cloves finely and scatter them over salads, serve them whole as antipasti, or nestle lots of them around a slowly roasting joint of lamb.

Garlic grows well – not just in the vegetable patch, but also in containers, tubs, and even flower borders, where it can help ward off aphids. New season's bulbs, with their soft white or purplish pink skins, are mild and sweet – and much better for pickling than older, drier-skinned garlic, which can be bitter.

Makes five 4-ounce jars

1 pound, 2 ounces new season's
  garlic bulbs
1 teaspoon fennel seeds
About 12 peppercorns (black, white,
  or pink)

4 to 6 bay leaves
³/₄ cup plus 2 tablespoons cider vinegar
¹/₄ cup granulated sugar
Good pinch of saffron threads

Bring a large pan of water to a boil. Plunge the garlic in for a mere minute, to help loosen the outer skins. Remove from the water, drain, and pat dry.

Have ready 3 warm, sterilized jars (see p. 21). Break the garlic bulbs into individual cloves. Peel the cloves and pack them into the jars, dropping in the fennel seeds, peppercorns, and bay leaves as you go.

Put the vinegar, sugar, and saffron into a pan. Bring to a boil and boil for a couple of minutes. Pour the hot vinegar over the garlic, then seal the jars with vinegar-proof lids (see p. 22). Use within 1 year.

P.S. There are two main types of garlic, hardneck and softneck. Hardnecks produce a flowering spike – or scape – which is usually snapped off to encourage the plant to put its energy into the bulb. These scapes have a delicate, fresh garlic flavor and can be used chopped up in salads or to make a green and garlicky pesto.

Pickled Florence fennel

Season: June to early July

Tall, willowy, feathered sweet Florence fennel, with its creamy-white, bulbous bottom, has to be one of the most alluring vegetables to grow in the garden. It's not easy to cultivate in every soil, but if it likes your particular situation, you should be able to grow plenty to use with gay abandon in the summertime, with some left over to preserve for later in the year.

It's only really worth making this pickle if you have a supply of freshly harvested bulbs when they are pale green and tender. All too often, the imported stuff is yellow and coarse. You have to discard much of the outer bulb, and it certainly isn't worth the expense or trouble of pickling.

This lovely light pickle is delicious with smoked or oily fish and in winter salads. It nearly always makes an appearance at our Boxing Day lunch.

Makes three to four 8-ounce jars

Salt
2¼ pounds fennel bulbs, trimmed and thinly sliced, a few feathery fronds reserved
4¼ cups cider vinegar
½ ounce peppercorns (black, white, or pink)
⅓ cup granulated sugar
Grated zest of 1 unwaxed lemon
3 or 4 bay leaves
1 teaspoon celery or fennel seeds
3 to 4 tablespoons olive, hempseed, or canola oil

Pour about 10 cups of water into a large pan, salt it well, and bring to a boil. Add the sliced fennel and blanch for no more than 1 minute. Drain in a colander, cool under cold water, then drain and pat dry.

Put the vinegar, peppercorns, sugar, lemon zest, bay leaves, and celery or fennel seeds into a saucepan. Bring to a boil and continue to boil for about 10 minutes, until the liquid reaches a syrupy consistency. The vinegar vapors will create quite a pungent atmosphere in the kitchen.

Pack the fennel into wide-necked, sterilized jars (see p. 21), lacing a few fennel fronds between the slices. Remove the vinegar syrup from the heat and carefully pour it over the fennel. You may well find all the spices remain at the bottom of the pan. If this happens, distribute them between the jars, poking the peppercorns and bay leaves down through the fennel slices. Pour sufficient oil into each jar to seal the surface. Seal the jars with vinegar-proof lids (see p. 22). Use within 1 year.

Roasted sweet beet relish

Season: June to August

I love the sweet, earthy flavor of beets and I hate to see it swamped in strong-tasting vinegar, as so often happens. This light preserve is quite a different proposition: roasting the young roots really concentrates their robust flavor, while the sharp pungency of horseradish adds a liveliness to the sweet beet. Serve this summery relish alongside smoked mackerel. It's also fantastic in sandwiches with cold meats.

Makes four 8-ounce jars

For the roasted tomato purée
2^1/$_4$ pounds tomatoes
2 teaspoons sea salt
4 garlic cloves, peeled and sliced
^{1}/$_4$ cup olive oil

2^1/$_4$ pounds young, small beets, trimmed

Olive oil, for drizzling
1^1/$_4$ cups granulated sugar
^{2}/$_3$ cup red wine vinegar
2 tablespoons balsamic vinegar
1 large red onion, peeled and finely chopped
2 ounces freshly grated horseradish root (or pickled horseradish, see below)

Preheat the oven to 350°F. For the tomato purée, halve the tomatoes and place them, skin side down, on a baking sheet. Sprinkle with the salt, garlic, and olive oil. Roast for 1 hour on the bottom shelf of the oven, then remove. Press through a sieve or pass through a food mill to remove the skins and seeds – you'll end up with about 1^1/$_4$ cups of intensely flavored purée.

Meanwhile, put the beets into a baking dish and drizzle with a little olive oil. Roast, above the tomatoes, for 1 to 1½ hours (longer if necessary), until the skins are blistered, blackened, and loosened. Let cool a little before peeling. You'll find the skins will slide off easily. Coarsely grate the beets (a food processor makes this job easy).

Put the sugar, vinegars, onion, and horseradish into a large saucepan; bring to a boil and cook for 5 minutes. Stir in the tomato purée and cook for a couple minutes more. Finally, add the grated beets and cook for about 10 minutes, until thickened. Transfer to sterilized jars and seal with vinegar-proof lids (see pp. 21–22). Use within 1 year. Refrigerate once opened.

P.S. It's easy to pickle horseradish root. Just grate enough fresh root to fill a jam jar, sprinkle with 1 teaspoon of salt and 1 teaspoon of sugar, top up with cider vinegar, and seal with a lid. Use in sauces, dressings, and soups, and serve with roast beef.

Seasonal chutney

Season: June to October

This is essentially Hugh Fearnley-Whittingstall's classic Glutney, or River Cottage chutney, which first appeared in *The River Cottage Cookbook*. The fruit and vegetable chopping is time-consuming, but important. Whizzing everything up in a food processor would give a very different, sloppy-textured result.

Makes twelve to thirteen 8-ounce jars

For the spice bag

2 ounces fresh ginger, bruised

12 cloves

2 teaspoons black peppercorns

1 teaspoon coriander seeds

$2^1/_4$ pounds summer squash, peeled (if need be) and diced

$2^1/_4$ pounds green tomatoes or tomatillos, peeled and diced

1 pound, 2 ounces cooking apples, peeled, cored, and diced

1 pound, 2 ounces onions, peeled and diced

3 cups golden raisins

$2^1/_2$ cups light brown sugar

$2^1/_2$ cups cider vinegar or white wine vinegar

2 teaspoons dried chile flakes (optional)

Pinch of salt

Make your spice bag by tying up the spices in an 8-inch square of cheesecloth. Put this into a preserving pan with all the other ingredients and bring slowly to a boil, stirring occasionally. This will take awhile, as there will be lots in the pan, but don't hurry it.

Let the mixture simmer, uncovered, for 2½ to 3 hours – maybe even a bit more. You do not have to hover, hawk-eyed, over the pan, but do keep an eye on it and stir regularly to ensure it doesn't burn. It's ready when it is glossy, thick, rich in color and well reduced – but with the chunks of fruit and vegetables still clearly discernible. It is thick enough if, when you draw a wooden spoon through it, the chutney parts to reveal the bottom of the pan for a few seconds.

Pot the chutney while warm in sterilized jars (see p. 21). Pack down with the back of a spoon to remove any air pockets. Seal with vinegar-proof lids (see p. 22). Store in a cool, dark place for a couple of months to mature before using. Use within 2 years.

Variations

For each variation, use $2^1/_2$ cups of light brown sugar, $2^1/_2$ cups of cider vinegar or white wine vinegar, a pinch of salt, and 2 teaspoons of dried chile flakes (if using) and follow the basic method.

Gingered rhubarb and fig (spring)

For the spice bag

2 teaspoons yellow mustard seeds
2 teaspoons black peppercorns
2 ounces fresh ginger, bruised

3 pounds, 6 ounces rhubarb, trimmed
   and chopped
2^1/$_4$ pounds cooking apples, peeled,
   cored, and diced
1 pound, 2 ounces onions, peeled
   and diced
2^1/$_2$ cups dried figs, chopped and
   soaked overnight in the juice of
   3 large oranges with the grated zest
   of 2 oranges
3^1/$_2$ ounces crystallized ginger, chopped

Plum and pear (late summer)

For the spice bag

2 ounces fresh ginger, bruised
2 teaspoons yellow mustard seeds
2 teaspoons black peppercorns

2^1/$_4$ pounds plums, quartered
   and pitted
1 pound, 10 ounces pears, peeled,
   cored, and diced
1 pound, 10 ounces cooking apples,
   peeled, cored, and diced
1 pound, 2 ounces shallots, peeled
   and diced
1^1/$_2$ cups pitted prunes,
   coarsely chopped

Apricot and date (late summer)

For the spice bag

2 ounces fresh ginger, bruised
1 teaspoon cloves
1 teaspoon cumin seeds
1 teaspoon coriander seeds
2 teaspoons black peppercorns

1 pound, 2 ounces unsulfured dried
   apricots, chopped, soaked
   overnight, and drained
2^1/$_4$ pounds summer squash, peeled
   (if need be) and diced
1 pound, 2 ounces cooking apples,
   peeled, cored, and diced
1 pound, 2 ounces onions, peeled
   and diced
1^1/$_2$ cups pitted dates, chopped
1^1/$_2$ cups raisins

Pumpkin and quince (early autumn)

For the spice bag

2 teaspoons peppercorns
12 cloves
2 cinnamon sticks

2^1/$_4$ pounds peeled and deseeded
   pumpkin, diced
2^1/$_4$ pounds quince, peeled, cored,
   and diced
1 pound, 10 ounces cooking apples,
   peeled, cored, and diced
1 pound, 10 ounces red onions, peeled
   and diced
3 cups raisins
2 ounces freshly grated horseradish
   root

Nasturtium "capers"

Season: late July to September

After the vibrant trumpets of nasturtium flowers fade, you'll find underneath the foliage the knobbly green seed pods of the plant. They have a hot, peppery flavor and, when pickled, develop a taste very similar to that of true capers (the pickled flower buds of the Mediterranean *Capparis* plant). Collect the seed pods on a warm, dry day when all the flowers have wilted away. Gather only the green ones (sometimes they are red-blushed) and avoid any that are yellowing, as these will be dull and dry. The pods can also be used fresh to spice up salads or as an ingredient in piccalilli (see p. 106).

These feisty little pickled nasturtium seed pods are great in fish dishes and in herby, garlicky sauces. Try them in tartar sauce or add them to salads, especially with tomatoes. In fact, use them just as you would capers.

Makes two 4-ounce jars

2^1/$_2$ teaspoons salt
3^1/$_2$ ounces nasturtium seed pods
A few peppercorns (optional)

Herbs, such as dill sprigs, tarragon sprigs, or bay leaves (optional)
About 1 cup white wine vinegar

Make a light brine by dissolving the salt in 1^1/$_4$ cups of water. Put the nasturtium seed pods into a bowl and cover with the cold brine. Let stand for 24 hours.

Drain the seed pods and dry well. Pack them into small, sterilized jars (see p. 21) with, if you like, a few peppercorns and herbs of your choice. Leave room for ^{3}/$_8$ inch of vinegar at the top. Cover the pods with the vinegar and seal the jars with vinegar-proof lids (see p. 22). Store in a cool, dark place for a few weeks before eating. Use within 1 year.

P.S. To make nasturtium tartar sauce, simply mix 7 tablespoons of mayonnaise with 2 to 3 finely chopped green onions or 1 ounce of finely chopped white part of a leek, 1 tablespoon of coarsely chopped nasturtium capers, 1 heaping tablespoon of finely chopped parsley, a squeeze of lemon juice, and salt and pepper to taste. Serve the sauce with simple grilled or fried white fish; hot or cold salmon or trout; or a salad of freshly cooked baby beets, young fava beans, and arugula or other salad greens.

Sweet cucumber pickle

Season: July to September

This is a wonderful way to use up an abundance of cucumbers, be they long and uniform green, or the short, knobbly-skinned type. It's also very quick and easy to make if you use a food processor. This is not a true preserve, as the cucumbers are not brined and the pickle is very light, but it will keep well in the fridge for a couple of weeks in a sealed container.

I love this sweet condiment with all manner of salads and in sandwiches, but it's especially delectable with hot-smoked trout or salmon.

Makes two 12-ounce jars

2 1/4 pounds cucumbers
3 small onions, red or white
1 tablespoon chopped dill (optional)

1 1/4 cups granulated sugar
1 tablespoon salt
3/4 cup plus 2 tablespoons
cider vinegar

Using the slicing blade of a food processor or a very sharp knife, very finely slice the cucumbers. Peel the onions and slice them very thinly. Combine the cucumbers, onions, and dill, if using, in a large bowl.

Mix the sugar, salt, and vinegar and pour over the cucumbers and onions. Let stand overnight for the sweet and sour flavors to mix and mingle or, if this isn't possible, let stand for at least 3 hours before serving. Pack into a large airtight container or wide-necked jam jars. Store in the fridge and use within 2 weeks.

Variation

Creamy-white English winter celery makes a lovely sweet pickle, or you can use the more common green celery. Follow the recipe above, replacing the cucumber with 2 1/4 pounds of celery. Run a potato peeler lightly down the stalks to remove any tough ribs, then cut into sticks about 1 1/2 inches long (for crudités or dips) or chop into 1/2- to 3/4-inch chunks. Use sweet, mild red onions and season the pickle with celery salt and 1 teaspoon of caraway seeds. As celery does not contain as much water as cucumber, add 3/4 cup plus 2 tablespoons of water to the vinegar and sugar mixture.

Piccalilli

This traditional sweet vegetable pickle, Indian in origin, is the ultimate August preserve for me. The time to make it is when garden produce is at its peak and there is ample to spare. You can use almost any vegetable in the mix, but make sure you include plenty of things that are green and crisp. The secret of a really successful piccalilli is to use very fresh vegetables and to take the time to cut them into small, similar-sized pieces.

The recipe first treats the vegetables to a dry-brining, which helps to keep them really firm and crunchy, then bathes them in a smooth, hot mustard sauce.

Makes three to four 8-ounce jars

2^1/$_4$ pounds washed, peeled vegetables – select 5 or 6 from the following: cauliflower or romanesco cauliflower, green beans, cucumbers, zucchini, green or yellow tomatoes, tomatillos, carrots, small silver-skinned onions or shallots, peppers, nasturtium seed pods

3 tablespoons fine salt

^{1}/$_4$ cup cornstarch

5 teaspoons ground turmeric

5 teaspoons English mustard powder (see p. 202)

1^1/$_2$ tablespoons yellow mustard seeds

1 teaspoon crushed cumin seeds

1 teaspoon crushed coriander seeds

2^1/$_2$ cups cider vinegar

^{3}/$_4$ cup granulated sugar

2 tablespoons honey

Cut the vegetables into small, even bite-size pieces. Place in a large bowl and sprinkle with the salt. Mix well, cover the bowl with a tea towel, and leave in a cool place for 24 hours, then rinse with ice-cold water and drain thoroughly.

Blend the cornstarch, turmeric, mustard powder, mustard seeds, cumin seeds, and coriander seeds to a smooth paste with a little of the vinegar. Put the rest of the vinegar into a saucepan with the sugar and honey and bring to a boil. Pour a little of the hot vinegar over the blended spice paste, stir well, and return to the pan. Bring gently to a boil. Boil for 3 to 4 minutes to allow the spices to release their flavors into the thickening sauce.

Remove the pan from the heat and carefully fold the well-drained vegetables into the hot, spicy sauce. Pack the pickle into warm, sterilized jars and seal immediately with vinegar-proof lids (see pp. 21–22). Leave to mature (if you can) for 4 to 6 weeks before opening. Use within 1 year.

Runner bean pickle

Season: August to September

Runner beans are a bit of a love-or-hate vegetable and are often scorned in favor of other green beans. I do sympathize with those who don't eat them – we've all been served rubbery, graying old runners at some time or another and they're no fun at all. However, young tender green runner beans are altogether different, and this recipe is just perfect for these guys. It has been eaten and enjoyed by nearly everyone who has walked into my kitchen, so I hope that reproducing it here will convert a few more bean haters. I think pickled beans are great alongside cold meats and salads.

Use a couple of jars that are at least 5 inches high – taller, if possible – so that the beans can show off their length.

Makes two 12-ounce jars

2¹/₄ pounds young runner beans
Salt
1¹/₄ cups cider vinegar or
   white wine vinegar
1¹/₂ cups granulated sugar
1 teaspoon ground allspice
1 teaspoon coarsely ground
   black pepper
6 juniper berries (optional)

Start by trimming the ends off the runner beans. If the beans are young and tender, there should be no need to string them. Cut the beans into lengths about ¹/₄ inch less than the height of the jar you are using.

Bring a pan of lightly salted water to a boil. Add the beans and cook until tender; this should take 5 to 8 minutes.

Meanwhile, put the vinegar, sugar, 7 tablespoons of water, the allspice, ground pepper, and juniper berries, if using, into a pan over low heat, stirring until the sugar has dissolved. Bring to a boil and boil for a couple of minutes. Drain the runner beans, immediately add them to the spiced vinegar, and simmer for 4 to 5 minutes. Strain the vinegar mixture into a small saucepan.

Pack the beans, upright, into warm, sterilized jars (see p. 21); kitchen tongs and a knife are useful for doing this. Return the spiced vinegar to a boil, then pour it over the tightly packed beans. Cap immediately with vinegar-proof lids (see p. 22).

Store in a cool, dark place for several weeks to allow the pickle to mature. Use within 1 year.

Sweet pickled damsons

Season: late August to September

Dark-skinned with a bluish bloom, small oval damson plums are very tart and well flavored, which makes them wonderful for preserving. This is a straightforward recipe that keeps the fruit whole and tender. I love warming cinnamon and allspice in the mix, but you can use any spices you fancy, or even a good tablespoonful of ready-made pickling spice (see p. 89). These sweet spiced damsons are a lovely addition to any buffet table and splendid with cold poultry.

Makes four 12-ounce jars

2^1/$_2$ cups cider vinegar
1 (2-inch) piece of cinnamon stick
1 teaspoon allspice berries
Juice and finely grated zest of 1 orange

2^1/$_4$ pounds firm, ripe damson plums or any other small, tart variety of plum
3^3/$_4$ cups granulated sugar

Put the vinegar, cinnamon, allspice berries, and orange juice and zest into a pan and bring to a boil. Boil for 4 to 5 minutes, then strain and allow to cool.

Prick each plum with a needle or skewer (this will prevent them from splitting). Add the fruit to the cool spiced vinegar in a clean pan. Bring slowly to a simmer, then simmer very, very gently for 10 to 15 minutes, until the plums are just tender. Using a slotted spoon, lift out the plums and pack them into warm, sterilized jars (see p. 21).

Return the spiced vinegar to the heat, add the sugar, and stir until dissolved. Boil for several minutes to reduce and thicken. Pour this hot spiced syrup over the plums and seal immediately with vinegar-proof lids (see p. 22). Store in a cool, dark place. These pickled damsons are best kept for 6 to 8 weeks before eating. Use within 1 year.

Variations

You can use the same method to pickle firm cherries or green gooseberries. Rhubarb, cut into 2-inch chunks, can also be dealt with in this way – but add the sugar with the rhubarb, as it will help keep it whole.

Spiced pickled pears

Season: August to December

I love pickled fruits and always look forward to opening a jar to serve with cold poultry and ham. Small, hard pears are ideal for use in this recipe, and it's a very good way to deal with a barrel-load of them. If you stick with the basic quantities of sugar and vinegar, this recipe can easily be adapted for use with other fruits and different spices (see the variations below).

Makes two to three 16-ounce jars

1¼ cups cider vinegar or white wine vinegar
2 cups granulated sugar
1 ounce fresh ginger, bruised

1 (2-inch) piece of cinnamon stick
1 teaspoon allspice berries
2¼ pounds small, firm pears
1 teaspoon cloves

Put the vinegar, sugar, ginger, cinnamon, and allspice berries into a large pan over low heat, stirring until the sugar has dissolved, then bring to a boil. Turn down the heat to a simmer.

Meanwhile, start peeling the pears, keeping them whole and with stems attached. Stud each pear with 2 or 3 cloves and add to the hot vinegar. Simmer the pears very gently for 15 to 25 minutes, until they are tender but not too soft. Remove with a slotted spoon and pack them into warm, sterilized jars (see p. 21).

Bring the spiced vinegar syrup to a boil and boil for 5 minutes, then strain it over the pears. Cover the jars with vinegar-proof lids (see p. 22). Keep for at least 1 month before using. Use within 1 year.

Variations

Different spices can be used – try cardamom and coriander, with a flake or two of dried chile.

Pickled peaches Plunge 2¼ pounds of peaches into a pan of boiling water for 1 minute, then remove. Immerse them in cold water briefly, then peel. Proceed as for the pear recipe, but simmer the peaches for only 3 to 4 minutes.

Pickled crab apples Prick 2¼ pounds of crab apples all over with a needle or skewer (this will prevent the skins bursting). Use well-colored ornamental varieties.

Pickled onions

Season: September to November

A good pickled onion is perhaps the doyen of the preserves cupboard – but how do you like yours? Crisp or soft, sweet or sour, mildly spiced or chile hot? The beauty of this recipe is that it can be used to make your onions (or shallots) just the way you like them. I like mine sweet, so I use honey in this recipe, but you could dispense with honey or sugar altogether if you like a really sharp pickle. I also go for cider vinegar, rather than the more traditional malt, because the flavor is less aggressive. The blend of spices used here suits me nicely, but you could also use coriander, cumin, or celery seeds – or any other spice you fancy. If you want crisp onions, use cold vinegar; if you like them soft, heat the vinegar first.

Makes one 24-ounce jar

2¹/₄ pounds small pickling onions	2 or 3 mace blades
3 tablespoons fine salt	2 teaspoons yellow mustard seeds
2¹/₂ cups vinegar (cider, malt, or wine)	1 teaspoon black or white peppercorns
7 tablespoons honey, or ³/₄ cup sugar	1 cinnamon stick
¹/₂ ounce fresh ginger, lightly bruised	2 dried chiles (optional)
2 teaspoons allspice berries	2 bay leaves

Using scissors, snip the top and the rooty bottom off the onions. Place in a large bowl and cover with boiling water. Count steadily to 20 (no more). Drain the onions and plunge into cold water. You will find the skins will peel off easily.

Put the peeled onions into a shallow dish. Sprinkle with the salt, cover, and let stand overnight. Meanwhile, pour the vinegar into a pan and add the honey or sugar, ginger, and spices (not the bay leaves). Cover and bring to a boil. Remove from the heat and allow to infuse overnight.

Strain the spiced vinegar. Rinse the onions in very cold water, then drain and pack into a sterilized jar (see p. 21), adding the bay leaves as you go. Pour in the vinegar (reheating it first if you want softer onions) and seal with a vinegar-proof lid (see p. 22). Let mature for 6 to 8 weeks before using. Use within 1 year.

Variation

Use shallots instead of onions and 1¹/₄ cups each of red wine vinegar and white wine vinegar. Prepare as above, then pack the shallots into the jar along with 1 ounce of sliced fresh ginger, 1 teaspoon of coriander seeds, and a couple of fresh mint sprigs.

Hearty ale chutney

Season: October to January

Spices, onions, and a traditional malty ale give this robust, pub-style chutney plenty of character, while the natural sugars in the root vegetables help sweeten it. It is delicious served with farmhouse Cheddar, crusty bread, and a pint or two.

Makes five to six 8-ounce jars

14 ounces onions, peeled and finely sliced

9 ounces rutabaga, peeled and chopped into $1/4$-inch pieces

7 ounces carrots, peeled and chopped into $1/4$-inch pieces

9 ounces apples, peeled, cored, and chopped into $2^1/2$-inch pieces

5 ounces cauliflower, broken into tiny florets

2 fat garlic cloves, peeled and crushed

$2/3$ cup pitted dates, finely chopped

$1/2$ cup plus 1 tablespoon tomato paste

$1^1/2$ cups Demerara sugar

$1/4$ cup dark muscovado sugar

1 cup malt or cider vinegar

2 heaping tablespoons English mustard powder (see p. 202)

2 heaping teaspoons ground ginger

1 heaping teaspoon ground mace

1 heaping teaspoon salt

½ teaspoon ground black pepper

1 pint traditional ale, bitter, or stout (not lager)

Put all the ingredients except the ale into a large pan with $2^1/4$ cups of water. Mix well, then place over low heat and bring to a gentle simmer, stirring until the sugar has dissolved. Cook for about 1 hour – the vegetables and fruit will begin to soften and the juices will thicken and reduce.

Take the pan off the heat and add half of the ale. Return to the heat and continue to cook for 30 minutes, by which time the mixture should be deep red-brown in color. Add the remaining ale and cook for a further 30 minutes. By now the vegetables and fruit should be tender but still retain their shape and a bit of crunch.

Remove from the heat and spoon into warm, sterilized jars (see p. 21), making sure there are no air pockets. Seal with vinegar-proof lids (see p. 22). Store for 4 to 6 weeks before opening. Use within 2 years.

Figgy mostardo

Season: autumn to winter

The Italians use fiery-hot mustard oil to add a bit of passion to their classic fruit preserve *mostardo di cremona*. However, mustard oil is pretty well impossible to purchase in this country, so I have used mustard seeds and powder to pep up the dried figs in my own interpretation of the dish. Serve it with hot or cold meat, with oily fish dishes, or with cheese in sandwiches.

Makes three 8-ounce jars

4 cups dried figs
Finely grated zest and juice of
    2 large grapefruit
1 heaping tablespoon yellow
    mustard seeds

1 cup granulated sugar, or $^2/_3$ cup
    honey
$^1/_4$ cup English mustard powder
    (see p. 202)
7 tablespoons cider vinegar or white
    wine vinegar

Cut each fig into 4 or 6 pieces – it's easiest to do this using scissors. Place the figs in a bowl and add the grapefruit zest and mustard seeds. Measure the grapefruit juice and add water if needed to reach 2 cups plus 2 tablespoons of liquid. Pour over the figs. Cover and let stand overnight.

Put the figs and juice into a heavy saucepan. Heat gently until simmering, then add the sugar or honey. Stir until dissolved.

Meanwhile, blend the mustard powder with the vinegar, add to the simmering figs, and stir well. Simmer, uncovered, for 20 minutes, stirring occasionally, to reduce and thicken.

Remove the pan from the heat. Spoon the *mostardo* into warm, sterilized jars and seal with vinegar-proof lids (see pp. 21–22). Store for 1 month before opening. Use within 1 year.

Variations

Dried apricots, apples, or pears, or a good mix of them all, can be used in place of figs. For a stronger, hotter *mostardo*, use black mustard seeds instead of the milder yellow seeds. Orange, lemon, or lime juice can replace the grapefruit juice. So you see, you can really make this recipe your very own.

Onion marmalade

Season: winter

Onions are one of the most versatile ingredients in the culinary world, but they are not often given the chance to be the star of their own show. A recipe like this puts that right. Long, slow cooking turns a panful of red, white, or yellow onions into a fantastic rich sauce-cum-jam that's brilliant served with sausages and mashed potatoes, and a heap of other dishes too. Try it with cheese on toast or with cold meat in sandwiches, or stir a spoonful into a creamy pumpkin soup.

Makes four 8-ounce jars

7 tablespoons olive oil
4¹/₂ pounds onions, peeled and
    finely sliced
1 cup Demerara sugar
7 tablespoons red currant jelly

1¹/₄ cups cider vinegar
¹/₄ cup balsamic vinegar
1 heaping teaspoon salt
¹/₂ teaspoon ground black pepper

Heat the oil in a large pan over medium heat and add the onions. Lower the heat, cover the pan, and cook over low heat, stirring occasionally, for 30 to 40 minutes, until the onions are collapsed and beginning to color.

Add the sugar and jelly. Increase the heat and continue to cook, stirring more frequently, for about 30 minutes, until the mixture turns a dark, nutty brown and most of the moisture has been driven off.

Take off the heat and allow to cool for a couple of minutes before adding the vinegars (if you add vinegar to a red-hot pan, it will evaporate in a fury of scorching steam). Return to the heat and cook rapidly for another 10 minutes or so, until the mixture becomes gooey and a spoon drawn across the bottom of the pan leaves a clear track on the bottom for a couple of seconds.

Remove from the heat and season with the salt and pepper. Spoon into warm, sterilized jars and seal with vinegar-proof lids (see pp. 21–22). Use within 1 year.

P.S. Marmalade is customarily made from citrus fruit; this marmalade is the exception to the rule. It takes its origins from the French, where historically the name *marmalade* was used to describe fruit that was cooked for a very long time until it was reduced to a thick purée.

Preserved lemons

Preserved lemons have a strong association with Middle Eastern and North African cuisines, and their unique zesty, salty yet mellow flavor permeates many of the traditional meat and couscous dishes of those regions. Strips of preserved lemon can also be added to salads, soups, and dressings, or mixed with olives and other appetizers. They are exceptionally easy to prepare, and I like to make them around the turn of the year when the new season's lemons from Spain and Italy are in the shops.

Makes two 12-ounce jars

2¹/₄ pounds small, ripe, unwaxed lemons

¹/₂ cup good-quality sea salt

1 teaspoon black or pink peppercorns

3 to 4 bay leaves

1 teaspoon coriander seeds (optional)

Wash the lemons in cold water and pat them dry. Set 4 of them aside – these will be squeezed and their juice poured over the salted lemons.

Using a sharp knife, partially quarter the remaining lemons lengthwise by making two deep cuts right through the fruit, keeping them intact at one end. Rub a good teaspoonful of salt into the cut surfaces of each lemon. Pack the fruit chock-a-block into sterilized, wide-necked jars (see p. 21), sprinkling in the remaining salt, and the peppercorns, bay leaves, and coriander seeds (if using) as you go.

Squeeze the juice from the reserved lemons and pour over the salted lemons. They must be completely covered. You can top up the jars with a little water if necessary. Seal with a vinegar-proof lid (see p. 22). Leave for at least 1 month to allow the lemon rinds to soften before opening.

To use, remove a lemon from the jar and rinse it well. Scoop out and discard the flesh (or purée it for use in dressings) and use the salted rind whole, chopped, or sliced. Make sure the lemons in the jar remain covered with liquid and, once opened, keep the jar in the fridge. Use within 1 year.

Cordials, Fruit
Liqueurs & Vinegars

Preserving the essences of fruits, flowers, and herbs by
steeping them in alcohol, vinegar, or a sugar syrup is the core of these recipes. You
might find yourself getting a bit bottled up in this chapter, but don't worry, you'll
find it very refreshing and in parts quite intoxicating. Many of the techniques are
age-old but are also enjoying a bit of a revival these days – fruit vinegars, in particular,
are becoming increasingly popular. Let me take you on a quick tour of the delicious
liqueurs and infusions in this chapter.

Cordials and fruit syrups Essentially, these are concentrated fruity syrups.
They are made from strained fruit juice sweetened with sugar. Some herbs
and flowers, such as elderflowers, can also be used in a similar way. These
smooth infusions can be diluted to taste (usually one part syrup to four or
five parts water) to make delicious still or fizzy drinks, or added slowly (to
prevent curdling) to ice-cold milk or yogurt to create shakes and smoothies.
Diluted half and half with water and frozen in suitable molds, they make
delicious ice pops. They can also be drizzled neat over ice cream for a quick
and easy dessert.

Flavored vinegars These are very simply made by steeping fruits, herbs, or
spices in vinegar. The vinegar is then strained (and the flavoring discarded)
and usually sweetened. Flavored vinegars can be used in dressings and
mayonnaises, sauces, relishes, pickles, and chutneys. They can be trickled
neat over a salad, grilled cheese, or avocado; diluted with ice-cold water to
make a refreshing summer drink (these can be very good); or sipped in the
winter to soothe sore, tickly throats. Fruit vinegars are usually made from
soft fruits such as raspberries, strawberries, or blackberries, which give up
their juices easily.

Fruit liqueurs If immersed in alcohol and left in a warm place for several
weeks, berries, fruit, scented leaves, and herbs will give up their flavors
beautifully. Sugar is often added to the mix too, during or after steeping, to
enhance the flavor. These tipples are not cheap to make, but I really value
them for their full, smooth flavors and find a small sip can spirit away
annoying thoughts.

Whole fruits in alcohol Raw or lightly cooked fruits can be preserved simply
by being sprinkled with sugar and submerged in alcohol. Such fruits make a
very special dessert, either on their own or served with a good vanilla ice
cream. Be assured that any liquor left after the fruit has been eaten is unlikely
to go to waste. . .

Key ingredients

You'll be amazed at how easily good fresh produce and simple pantry ingredients can be transformed into such wide-ranging and stimulating liquors.

Vinegar

Always use a good-quality vinegar with at least 5 percent acetic acid. Light and fruity cider or wine vinegars are best for flavoring. Use the vinegar cold if it's to be steeped with soft, fresh leaves and flowers, but heat it for the best results with firm ingredients such as garlic, chiles, and horseradish. For more on vinegars, see p. 29.

Sugar

Refined white sugar or unrefined granulated sugar is best in these recipes, to allow the flavors of the fruit, flowers, or herbs to prevail. For more information on sugars, see p. 27.

Alcohol

Alcohol is a very effective preserving medium but needs to be in the form of spirits with at least 40 percent alcohol (80 proof). See p. 30 for more information.

Fruit

Fruit must be fresh, of the highest quality, and definitely not underripe. In fact, fruit that is a little too ripe for jam or for canning is ideal for fruit syrups. Perfectly ripe fruit should be used for preserved whole fruits and fruit liqueurs – prick it with a needle or skewer in several places to help the juices flow. Only wash the fruit if absolutely necessary. Otherwise, prepare as follows:

> **Strawberries and raspberries** Remove the hull.
> **Cherries** Pit or not, it's up to you.
> **Peaches and apricots** Peel if you like, then slice or quarter.
> **Plums** Halve or leave whole. If leaving whole, prick with a fork or skewer.
> **Pears** Peel or not, then core and halve or quarter.
> **Grapes** Remove the stems.
> **Early blackberries** Pick over.

Herbs, spices, and flowers

It is important to gather herbs and flowers when they are fully dry and, ideally, when they have been gently warmed by the sun. This is when their characteristic oils and essences are at their best and most pungent. Likewise, spices and aromatics should be fresh and strong smelling.

Shelf life and keepability

Fruit vinegars and liqueurs are best used within 2 years, although providing they are well sealed and kept in a cool, dry place, they will keep for considerably longer. Fruit syrups and cordials have a shorter shelf life – they can be kept in a cool, dry place or the refrigerator for a few weeks, or frozen. You can, however, extend their shelf life as follows.

Extending shelf life of fruit syrups and cordials to 4 months Sterilize your bottles and their corks, swing-top lids, or screw-tops by putting them all in a large pan of water and bringing to a boil. Leave them in the pan so they are still hot when you are ready to use them.

Bring the fruit syrup to just above simmering (check that it reaches 190° to 195°F on a candy thermometer). Using a funnel, fill the hot bottles to within $^3/_8$ inch of the brim if you're using screw-tops or swing-stoppers, or within 1 inch of the brim if you're using corks. Fill each bottle and seal it before filling the next bottle. This method avoids using a deep-pan hot water bath (it is difficult to find a pan deep enough to fully submerge bottles).

Extending shelf life of fruit syrups and cordials to 1 year To do this, you need to process the filled bottles in a hot water bath (see p.156). Fill the bottles with syrup to within 1 inch of the tops for screw-tops or swing-top lids, and to within $1^3/_8$ inches of the tops if you are using corks – this allows for expansion and prevents the tops from blowing off. Screw-lids should be put on lightly and then tightened when the bottles are taken out of the water bath. Corks need to be held down and prevented from blowing off during the heating process by securing them with some strong insulation tape. Swing-tops should be fully sealed – the rubber ring will allow steam to escape.

Stand the filled, sealed bottles in a deep pan on a trivet or folded tea towel. Fill the pan with water to within 1 inch of the top of the bottles and bring to a simmer (190°F). Keep at this temperature for 20 minutes. Remove from the pan and let cool.

Once cold, bottles that have been sealed with a cork can be made airtight by dipping the cork and the top $^3/_8$ inch of the bottle into melted paraffin wax or beeswax.

Storage after opening Whichever method you choose, once opened, the bottles should be kept in the fridge.

Family 'beena

Season: pretty much all year round

I'd like to introduce you to a group of cordials with a name inspired by a British fruit juice beverage called Ribena. These can be prepared throughout the year and are an excellent way of using fruit that's too ripe for jam making. I've made rhubeena with rhubarb, berrybeena with summer berries, plumbeena with plums – and currants work very well too. Use these fruits alone to make single-variety 'beenas or, for a lighter and more economical cordial, use 50 percent cooking apples.

Because the fruit pulp will be strained, you needn't be too fastidious with its preparation. Rhubarb should be cut into chunks. Strawberries should be hulled. Plums are best halved, but it's not necessary to remove the pits. Apples should be stemmed and coarsely chopped, but there's no need to peel or core them.

Makes about 6 cups
4¹/₂ pounds fruit
Granulated sugar
Brandy (optional)

Place your chosen prepared fruit in a large saucepan. For each pound of black currants, apples, or hard fruit, add 1 cup plus 2 tablespoons of water; for each pound of plums or stone fruit, add ¹/₂ cup plus 1 tablespoon of water; for each pound of soft berries or rhubarb, add 3 tablespoons of water. Bring slowly to a boil, crushing the fruit with a wooden spoon or potato masher, and cook gently until the fruit is soft and the juices flowing. This will take up to 45 minutes, depending on the type of fruit. Remove from the heat.

Suspend a jelly strainer bag or fine tea towel (see p. 33) over a large bowl. Pour the fruit into it and leave to drip overnight.

Measure the resulting juice and pour into a clean pan. For every 2 cups of juice, add 1³/₄ cups of sugar (or to taste). Heat the mixture gently to dissolve the sugar, then remove from the heat. Pour immediately into warm, sterilized bottles (see p. 125), leaving a ³/₈-inch gap at the top. At this point you may like to add a couple of teaspoonfuls of brandy to each bottle. Seal with a screw-top or cork.

'Beenas will keep for several months, provided they are sealed when hot and stored in a cool place. However, if you want to keep them for longer, you will need to sterilize the bottles in a water bath immediately after canning (see p. 125).

Lemon syrup

Season: November to March

A cool glass of homemade lemonade knocks the commercially produced alternative into oblivion. Once tasted, this will become a favorite thirst quencher. Serve this lemon syrup diluted with cold water as a cool summertime refresher, or mix with tonic water and a splash of Angostura bitters for a nonalcoholic cocktail. You can also use oranges as well as lemons.

Makes two to three 16-ounce bottles
7 **to 10 unwaxed lemons**
3¹/₄ **cups granulated sugar**

Scrub the lemons and pare the zest from 4 of them. Bring a pan of water to a boil, drop in all of the lemons, and leave for 1 minute. Lemons are often quite hard and unyielding – this will soften them, and they will give more juice when squeezed. Lift out the lemons and keep the lemon-infused water to one side. Squeeze the juice from the lemons and measure out 2 cups plus 2 tablespoons of it.

Put the sugar, lemon zest, and 2 cups plus 2 tablespoons of the lemon-infused water into a saucepan. Heat gently to dissolve the sugar, then bring to a boil. Add the lemon juice and bring just to the boiling point. Remove from the heat and strain through a sieve into a pitcher. Pour immediately into hot, sterilized bottles (see p. 125) and seal immediately with sterilized screw-caps, corks, or swing-top lids.

Let cool, then store in a cool, dry place or the fridge for up to 4 months. For longer keeping – up to 1 year – sterilize the filled bottles in a water bath (see p. 125).

To serve, mix 1 part syrup to 4 parts water.

P.S. Another way to increase the yield of juice from citrus fruits is to roll the fruit back and forth over a work surface, pressing down firmly with the palm of your hand, for 2 to 3 minutes.

Beech leaf noyau

Season: late April to early May

The name for this unusual alcoholic cordial is actually the French word for fruit pit. Traditionally, it was made from bitter almonds or peach pits mixed with gin and left to steep in a warm place for several days before being cooked up with sugar, and then filtered through blotting paper. This recipe is from Richard Mabey's excellent *Food for Free*. It uses the young, silken leaves of the European beech tree (*Fagus sylvatica*), to make an exquisite hedgerow version of the liqueur; the leaves first appear toward the end of April.

Makes 4 cups

1 loosely packed grocery bag full of soft young beech leaves, sufficient to pack tightly into a 2¹/₂- to 3-cup jar

2 cups gin
1¹/₂ cups granulated sugar
Brandy

Pack the beech leaves into an earthenware or glass jar until it's about nine-tenths full. Pour the gin over the leaves, making sure they are well covered (they will oxidize and turn brown if left exposed). Let steep for 7 to 10 days so the leaves can release their striking green pigment. Strain the infused gin through cheesecloth or a jelly strainer bag (see p. 33).

Put the sugar and 1 cup of water into a saucepan and heat gently to dissolve the sugar. Allow to cool completely before adding to the infused gin. Add a couple of capfuls of brandy too.

Put a couple of fresh beech leaves into a sterilized screw-top or stopper bottle (see p. 125), then add the noyau and seal.

Wait for a cold winter night and a roaring fire, then partake of this potent liqueur. Use within 2 years (it may darken in color over time).

P.S. If you miss the young beech leaves of early spring, you may get a second chance to make this noyau toward the end of June. Some beech hedges, when trimmed, will throw up new young shoots – not as prolific as the early crop, but still worth snatching.

Elderflower cordial

Season: late May to June

The sweetly scented, creamy-white flowers of the elder tree appear in abundance in hedgerows, scrublands, woodlands, and wastelands at the beginning of summer. The fresh flowers make a terrific aromatic cordial. They are best gathered just as the many tiny buds are beginning to open and some are still closed. Gather on a warm, dry day (never when wet), checking that the perfume is fresh and pleasing. Trees do differ, and you will soon get to know the good ones. Remember to leave some flowers to develop into berries for picking later in the year.

This recipe is based on one from the River Cottage archives; it's sharp and lemony and makes a truly thirst-quenching drink. You can, however, adjust it to your liking by adding more or less sugar. The cordial will keep for several weeks as is. If you want to keep it for longer, either add some citric acid and sterilize the bottles after filling (see p. 125), or pour into plastic bottles and store in the freezer.

Serve the cordial diluted with ice-cold sparkling or still water as a summer refresher – or mix with sparkling wine or Champagne for a classy get-together. Add a splash or two, undiluted, to fruit salads or anything with gooseberries – or dilute one part cordial to two parts water for fragrant ice lollies.

Makes about 8 cups

About 25 elderflower heads
Finely grated zest of 3 unwaxed lemons and 1 orange, plus their juice (about 2/3 cup in total)

5 cups granulated sugar
1 heaping teaspoon citric acid (optional)

Inspect the elderflower heads carefully and remove any insects. Place the flower heads in a large bowl together with the orange and lemon zest. Bring 6 1/2 cups of water to a boil and pour over the elderflowers and citrus zest. Cover and leave overnight to infuse.

Strain the liquid through a jelly strainer bag or piece of cheesecloth (see p. 33) and pour into a saucepan. Add the sugar, the lemon and orange juice, and the citric acid, if using. Heat gently to dissolve the sugar, then bring to a simmer and cook for a couple of minutes.

Use a funnel to pour the hot syrup into sterilized bottles (see p. 125). Seal the bottles with swing-top lids, sterilized screw-tops, or corks.

Elixir of sage

Season: spring and summer

The healing, warming properties of sage have long been recognized, and one traditional way to imbibe them is by means of a liqueur, such as this one. The velvety, gray-green leaves are steeped in eau-de-vie and the resulting elixir should, I'm told, be drunk each day to ensure good health and a long life. I take just a capful (not a cupful) myself each morning and find it very restorative. Of course, this is not the only way to use this soothing herb liqueur – a glassful can be enjoyed as a comforting digestif, or a capful can be diluted with tonic water for an aromatic pick-me-up.

Gather the sage on a warm, dry day. As an evergreen, this herb can be picked throughout the year, but it's at its best during the spring and summer months.

Makes 4 cups
2 to 2$^1/_2$ ounces sage leaves
About 2 cups eau-de-vie
1 cup granulated sugar

Shake the sage leaves well to remove any wildlife (those that don't escape at this stage will become sublimely intoxicated). Pack the leaves into a large, wide-necked 2$^1/_2$- to 3-cup jar. Fill the jar to the very top with eau-de-vie and seal with an airtight lid (if any leaves are uncovered, they will oxidize and the color of the liqueur will become dull brown). Give it a good shake and then place on a sunny windowsill to steep for about 1 month, remembering to give it a shake every now and then.

When you're ready to complete the elixir, make a sugar syrup by gently heating the sugar with $^3/_4$ cup plus 2 tablespoons of water until the sugar has dissolved. Allow this to cool.

Strain the sage liquor through a sieve into a bowl. Stir in the sugar syrup. Decant into sterilized bottles (see p. 125), placing 2 or 3 of the soaked sage leaves in each bottle. Cork or cap with screw-caps. The elixir is ready to use immediately. Use within 1 year.

Currant shrub

Season: June to July

A shrub is an old-fashioned kind of drink – essentially a delightfully fruity alcoholic cordial. Based on sweetened rum or brandy, it is traditionally flavored with acidic fruit such as Seville oranges, lemons, or red currants. Keep back some of the juice after straining red currants to make jelly (see recipe, p. 54), and you will find this lovely tipple very simple to make.

Serve as an aperitif, either on its own or mixed half and half with a dry martini and finished with a splash of fresh orange juice, which is my favorite way.

Makes about 4 cups
1¹/₄ cups strained red currant juice
2¹/₂ cups rum or brandy
Finely grated zest of 1 orange

1 teaspoon freshly grated nutmeg
1¹/₂ cups granulated sugar

Mix the red currant juice, rum or brandy, orange zest, and nutmeg together in a large, wide-necked jar. You may find the mixture of acid and alcohol forms a gel – a perfect example of how adding fruit juice to spirit can determine pectin levels (see pp. 38–39). Don't worry, the mixture will become liquid again when you add the sugar. Seal the jar tightly and leave for 7 to 10 days in a cool, dark place.

Transfer the currant and alcohol mixture to a pan, add the sugar, and heat gently to about 140°F. When the sugar has dissolved, strain the liqueur through a jelly strainer bag or cheesecloth (see p. 33). Decant the strained liquid into a sterilized bottle (see p. 125) and seal with a cap.

Store for several months in a cool, dark place so the shrub can fully mature before you take the first tipple. Use within 2 years.

P.S. Red currants that grow on a standard (long-stemmed) bush, rather than at ground level, make picking very easy and also add interest to the garden. I pick about 10 pounds of red currants each season from my standard bush.

Variation
At marmalade-making time, buy an extra couple of pounds of Seville oranges and use the strained juice in place of the red currant juice for an outstanding orange liqueur.

Mint syrup

I can't help feeling that we should all make more use of garden mint. I'm sure that if it didn't run amok in the garden in a rather annoying way, we would prize it more highly not just as a nice thing to chuck in with the potatoes, but as the wonderful sweet-scented herb that it is.

This simple recipe is best made with young, bright green mint leaves picked just before flowering, when the volatile oils are at their strongest. Gather them on a sunny day, when the plant is fully dry and the leaves are warm. Use the leaves immediately after picking to retain every bit of their amazing warming and cooling menthol character.

Mix 2 teaspoons of mint syrup into a glass of ice-cold water, lemonade, or tonic for a cooling summer drink. To make delicious hot, sweet mint tea, add 1 tablespoon of the syrup to a pot (silver, of course, if you have one) of steaming green tea.

Makes 4 cups

2 ounces freshly picked mint leaves	1¼ cups granulated sugar
Juice of 1 lemon	1 teaspoon sea salt

Check the mint leaves for any insect life, then tear the leaves into shreds. Put the lemon juice into a large bowl. Add the mint and pound with the end of a wooden rolling pin. Add the sugar and salt and continue to crush the mint leaves to release their menthol essence. Leave to macerate for 8 to 10 hours or overnight.

Pour 2½ cups of boiling water over the macerated mint mixture and let stand for a further 12 hours.

Strain the syrup through a very fine sieve or cheesecloth into a saucepan. Gently bring to a simmer and simmer for a couple of minutes. Pour into warm, sterilized bottles (see p. 125) and seal with screw-caps or corks.

This syrup will keep unopened for 4 months, but once opened, it should be stored in the fridge. If you want to keep it longer, it will need to be sterilized in a water bath straight after canning (see p. 125).

Flavored vinegars

Season: June to November

These are very useful additions to the pantry as their distinctive flavors can revolutionize a simple salad dressing or sauce. The process is simple: aromatic herbs, flowers, or strong-flavored ingredients are steeped in vinegar for a period of time and are then strained out. The vinegar is then decanted into a sterilized bottle and sealed (see p. 125).

Always pick leaves and flowers for steeping when they are dry and their perfume is at its best. Use cider vinegar or white wine vinegar – or perhaps try some delicate rice vinegar to give a hint of Asian flavor to the mix.

Horseradish vinegar

Peel and grate 2 ounces of freshly dug horseradish root and pack into a large sterilized jar with 2 finely chopped shallots, 1 teaspoon of sugar, and ½ teaspoon of salt. Heat 2¹/₂ cups of cider vinegar to just below boiling and pour over the mix. Seal and store for a month or so before straining and bottling. I like to use this vinegar for pickling cucumbers or beets.

Nasturtium vinegar

Fill a wide-necked 20-ounce jar with freshly gathered, brilliantly colored nasturtium flowers, a few spicy nasturtium seed pods (see p. 103), 2 chopped shallots, 8 to 10 peppercorns, and ½ teaspoon of salt. Pour in 2 cups of cold white wine vinegar. Store for a month or so in a sunny spot, giving the jar a shake every now and then. Strain the vinegar and discard the flowers. Pack into a sterilized jar with a couple of fresh nasturtium flowers to identify the vinegar.

To make a splendid summer salad dressing, add 1 tablespoon of soy sauce to ¹/₂ cup of nasturtium vinegar and whisk in 1 cup of olive or canola oil.

Mixed herb vinegar

Mix a heaping ¹/₄ cup of herbs – chives, parsley, tarragon, fennel, thyme, or whatever you have – with 2 cups of cold white wine vinegar or cider vinegar. Store for 3 to 4 weeks in a cool, dark place. Strain, discard the herbs, and bottle.

Spiced samphire vinegar

Pack 2 ounces of samphire, 6 allspice berries, and 2 finely chopped shallots into a large jar. Pour in 2 cups of cold rice vinegar or cider vinegar. Store for 2 to 3 months before straining and bottling. This is great with fish and in sweet-and-sour sauces.

Raspberry vinegar

Historically, sweetened vinegars were valued for their medicinal qualities and were typically used to relieve coughs and treat fevers and colds. During the nineteenth century, raspberry vinegar in particular was recommended as a refreshing tonic to overcome weariness. But fruit vinegars have a multitude of culinary uses too, and I certainly wouldn't want to be without a bottle or two in the kitchen.

Use raspberry vinegar on salads – either neat or blended with olive oil. I also love it trickled over goat's cheese, crepes, and even ice cream. You'll also find that a spoonful adds a lovely piquancy to savory sauces. For a revitalizing summer drink, mix a couple of tablespoonfuls of raspberry vinegar with soda or tonic water and add ice.

The fruit for a vinegar needs to be gathered on a dry day. If the fruit is wet, it will dilute the vinegar and adversely affect its keeping quality.

Makes 6 cups
2$^1/_4$ pounds raspberries
2$^1/_2$ cups cider vinegar or white wine vinegar
Granulated sugar

Put the raspberries in a bowl and crush them lightly with a wooden spoon. Add the vinegar. Cover the bowl and let the fruit and vinegar steep for 4 to 5 days, stirring occasionally.

Pour the fruit and vinegar into a jelly strainer bag or piece of cheesecloth suspended over a bowl (see p. 33) and let drain overnight. You can squeeze it a little if you like.

Measure the liquid, then pour into a saucepan. For every cup of fruit vinegar, add 1 cup of sugar. Place over low heat and bring gently to a boil, stirring until the sugar has dissolved. Boil for 8 to 10 minutes, removing any scum as it rises. Remove from the heat and let cool, then bottle and seal (see p. 125). Use within 1 year.

Variations
Replace the raspberries with the same quantity of strawberries, black currants, or blackberries to create other fruit vinegars.

Rosehip syrup

Season: late September to October

The shapely rosehip is the fleshy fruit of the rose. The orange-red berries that appear in the autumn contain a crowd of creamy-white seeds protected by tiny irritant hairs, which is why they should never be eaten raw. Rosehips are rich in vitamins A and C and have long been used for making jams, jellies, wine, tea, and, of course, syrup. This recipe is based on one issued by the British Ministry of Defence during the Second World War when rosehips were gathered by volunteers. The syrup made from the fruit was fed to the nation's children.

Use this rosehip syrup mixed with hot water as a warming winter drink. I also love it drizzled neat over rice pudding or pancakes. Or try this recipe of Hugh Fearnley-Whittingstall's for a refreshing summer cocktail: pour 2 tablespoons of rosehip syrup into a tall glass. Add $^1/_4$ cup of white rum and mix well. Add a few ice cubes and pour in about $^2/_3$ cup of tart apple juice. Garnish with a sprig of mint and serve with a straw.

Makes about 6 cups
1 pound, 2 ounces rosehips (see p. 202)
3$^1/_4$ cups granulated sugar

Pick over the rosehips, removing the stems, and rinse in cold water.

Put 3$^1/_3$ cups of water in a pan and bring to a boil. Meanwhile, mince the rosehips or chop them in a food processor. Add them to the pan of boiling water, cover, and bring back to a boil. Take off the heat and let stand for 15 minutes. Pour through a jelly strainer bag or piece of cheesecloth (see p. 33) and let drip for an hour.

Set aside the strained juice. Bring another 3$^1/_3$ cups of water to a boil, add the rosehip pulp, and repeat the boiling process. Pour the mixture back into the jelly strainer bag or cheesecloth and this time leave to drain overnight.

The next day, combine both batches of strained juice (you can discard the rosehip pulp). Measure the juice (you should have about 4 cups) and pour into a saucepan. Add the sugar and heat, stirring until dissolved. Boil for 2 to 3 minutes, then immediately pour into warm, sterilized bottles (see p. 125) and secure with screw-caps or corks.

Use within 4 months. If you want to keep the syrup for longer, you'll need to sterilize the bottles in a water bath (see p. 125).

Sloe gin

Season: September to October

This is undoubtedly the best-known of the English hedgerow liqueurs. The sloe, or blackthorn, is a small, black, mouth-puckering plum that is native to Britain but rare in the United States. If you are unable to obtain it, any other small, tart plum will do. If your plums are quite sweet, reduce the amount of sugar, or try some of my other favorite variations on this theme (below). There is no reason why you cannot use vodka instead of gin.

Makes about 4 cups
1 pound sloes, frozen or pricked all over with a skewer
2$^{1}/_{4}$ cups granulated sugar (or less for a more tart gin)
2$^{1}/_{2}$ cups gin

Put the sloes into a large clean jar or bottle. Pour in the sugar, followed by the gin. Secure the container with the lid and give it a good shake to mix up the contents. Shake daily for the next week to prevent the sugar from settling on the bottom and to help release the sloe juice. Thereafter, shake and taste once a week for 8 to 10 weeks.

When the sloes have instilled their flavor, pass the mixture through a fine sieve. Pour the strained liqueur into bottles.

Ideally, you should store sloe gin for 18 months before drinking, so it pays to have a year's batch in hand. Of course, that's not always possible – but do try and stash a bottle or two away to savor when it's mature and mellow.

And what to do with all those gin-soaked sloes? You can either eat them just as they are, or remove the pits and serve the fruit with ice cream or fold them into melted chocolate to make delectable petits fours.

Variations

In each case, follow the method for sloe gin, but with the following quantities:

Damson gin Use 1 pound of damson plums, pricked, 1 cup of sugar, and 2$^{1}/_{2}$ cups of gin.

Blackberry and apple gin Use 8 ounces of blackberries, 8 ounces of cooking apples (peeled and chopped), 1 cup of sugar, and 2$^{1}/_{2}$ cups of gin.

Cherry ratafia Use 1 pound, 2 ounces of cherries, pricked, 2 cups plus 2 tablespoons of eau-de-vie, 2 cinnamon sticks, and $^3/_4$ cup of vanilla sugar.

Haw brandy Use 1 pound of hawthorn berries, 1 cup of sugar, and $2^1/_2$ cups of brandy.

Bachelor's jam

Season: June to October

This is also known as officer's jam, but it's really not a jam at all. The German name, *Rumtopf*, seems far more appropriate for what is actually a cocktail of rum-soaked fruit. The idea is that the mixture of fruit, alcohol, and sugar is added to gradually, as different fruits ripen throughout the growing season. This preserve is usually prepared with Christmas in mind, when the potent fruity alcohol is drunk and the highly spirited fruit can be served on its own or with ice cream and desserts.

You will need a large glazed stoneware or earthenware pot with a closely fitting lid and a small plate, saucer, or other flat object that will fit inside the pot and keep the fruit submerged.

Fruit in season (see p. 124 for preparation)
4 to 8 cups rum, brandy, vodka, or gin (40 proof)
Granulated sugar (1 cup plus 2 tablespoons per pound of fruit)

Choose just-ripe fruits as they appear through the summer and fall. I normally kick off the pot with some of the first sweet strawberries of the season. Place these in the bottom of your pot and, for every pound of fruit, sprinkle over 1 cup plus 2 tablespoons of sugar. Leave this for an hour or so, then pour in about 4 cups of your chosen alcohol. Place the saucer on top of the fruit to make sure the fruit remains immersed. Then cover the pot with plastic wrap and, finally, a close-fitting lid.

Carry on like this throughout the summer and autumn, adding raspberries, cherries, peaches, plums, damson plums, pears, grapes, and blackberries as they come into season. (I avoid currants and gooseberries because their skins tend to toughen in the alcohol syrup, and I find rhubarb is too acid for the pot.) Add the sugar each time too, and keep topping up the alcohol so that it always covers the fruit by about ³/₄ inch.

Do not stir the fruit at any point, just let it sit in its layers. When the pot is full to the brim, seal it tightly and store for a couple of months before you start enjoying the contents. Just prior to using, dig deep and give the contents a good stir to combine all the scrumptious flavors. Use within 1 year.

P.S. If you're in a hurry, you can make bachelor's jam in one go in August, when lots of different fruits should be available. However, I do find it more fun to add the fruit over several months, whenever I have a surplus.

Canned Fruits

With the advent of the deep-freeze, canning

has rather slipped from necessity and fashion. That's a shame, as it is an excellent way of preserving fruits – far better than freezing for some, such as peaches, cherries, figs, and apricots. These, when canned, will remain closer in flavor and texture to their natural state. Another advantage of canning is that the fruit is ready and waiting to be used at any moment – there's none of that ferreting about in the bottom of the freezer or waiting for a soggy mass of fruit to defrost.

Nevertheless, unraveling the canning process can seem like cracking a secret code. There are so many methods to choose from – the slow water method, the quick water method, the very low oven, the moderate oven, or the pressure cooker – as well as charts to navigate. To make it easier and to encourage you to have a go, I have whittled down canning to two basic methods – the water bath method and the oven method. To be successful, both rely on two simple points – the fruit must be sterilized by heating, and the jars must be perfectly sealed.

Jars and bottles

The containers used for canning are stronger than normal jam jars because they need to withstand a heating process. Two types are generally used (see below) and both are available in half-pint, pint, quart, and half-gallon (8-, 16-, 32-, and 64-fluid ounce) sizes.

The jars, lids, and rubber rings should be sterilized before the fruit is packed in. I find the easiest way to do this is to place them in a large pan of cold water and bring slowly to a boil. I then remove the pan from the heat and leave the jars in the water until I need them. Remove the jars from the pan with a pair of tongs. There is no need to dry the jars. Alternatively, before use, the jars can be washed in hot water, left inverted to drain, then put in a 275°F oven for 15 minutes.

Screw-band jars Often referred to as Mason jars, these have metal lids with a rubber seal that separates the top of the jar and the lid. The screw-band is fully tightened only after the cooking process, to seal the jar and form a vacuum. Lids cannot be reused; the built-in seal works one time only.

Lock-lid jars These have a rubber ring to separate the jar top from the jar lid but are fastened with a metal spring clip. These jars allow steam to escape, but no air can enter. They normally have a wider mouth than screw-band jars and are therefore more suitable for use with larger fruits, such as pears or peaches.

The rubber rings must be a perfect fit and in perfect condition – so check them before using. They will deteriorate with use and will need replacing from time to time. The rubber rings can either be sterilized with the jars and lids, or be soaked in warm water (100°F) for 15 minutes (this makes it much easier to stretch them on), then dipped in boiling water just before they go on the jar.

Preparing syrup

Fruit can be canned in plain water, but a syrup based on sugar or honey will improve the flavor. Alcohol, pure fruit juice, fruit cordials, scented leaves, and spices can be added to give character and interest. The strength of the syrup depends on the type of fruit used and how you like your fruit to taste – the tarter the fruit, the heavier you'll want to make the syrup. Generally, you want a sweeter syrup for more tightly packed fruit too, because less is used. Syrups are always prepared by simply dissolving the required amount of sugar or honey in water and boiling for 1 minute.

Light syrup 3 tablespoons sugar (2 tablespoons honey), 1 cup water
Medium syrup $^1/_3$ cup sugar (3 tablespoons honey), 1 cup water
Heavy syrup $^1/_2$ cup sugar ($^1/_4$ cup honey), 1 cup water

Fruit for canning

Fruit should ideally be perfectly ripe, but err on the side of under rather than over if you have to. Handle the fruit carefully as any bruising will spoil the preserves. Prepare it by removing stalks, stems, leaves, and hulls and rinsing in cold water if necessary. Vegetables require a very high-temperature process and are not suitable for home canning by either of the methods covered in this book.

Plums and cherries These can be canned whole or pitted – pits will impart an agreeable almondy flavor. There's no need to prick the fruit.

Gooseberries These are best canned when green and slightly underripe. The skins should be pricked or nicked to prevent shriveling.

Pears and apples These should be peeled and cored before canning. Pears can be cored and quartered or left whole. Once peeled, place in a bowl of salted water ($1^1/_2$ tablespoons of salt to 4 cups of water) to prevent discoloration until ready to pack.

Peaches, apricots, and nectarines These should be peeled: immerse in boiling water for 1 minute, then plunge into cold water, peel, and pack immediately.

Rhubarb These stalks should be chopped into 1- to 2-inch lengths and steeped overnight in a light to medium syrup prior to packing and processing.

Soft fruits Handle these as little as possible – just remove stems or hulls.

Packing tips

Fruit to be canned should be handled as little as possible. Packing the fruit in neatly will mean you can get more in the jar.

1. Fruit will shrink during the heating process so should be packed into jars as tightly as possible, but without bruising.

2. Use a long-handled packing spoon, the end of a wooden spoon, or a chopstick to position fruit and tease out any air bubbles.

3. Stand jars on a wooden surface or newspaper when filling with hot syrup.

4. Make sure the rim of the jar is free from seeds or fruit fibers.

5. Give the jar a sharp knock or swirl to remove any trapped air before sealing.

The water bath method

For canning in a water bath, you need a pan deep enough to contain the jars completely submerged underwater. The jars will crack if they sit directly on the bottom of the pan, so it needs a "false bottom" such as a wire trivet or a folded tea towel. A thermometer is essential to check the temperature.

The fruit should be packed into jars and filled to the brim with hot syrup (about 140°F). If you're using Mason jars, the band should be released by a quarter of a turn for steam to escape. Place the jars in the pan and cover completely with warm water (100°F). Heat to the simmering point (190°F) over a period of 25 to 30 minutes, then simmer for the time given in the recipe or in the chart on p. 159.

Remove the jars one at a time and place them on a wooden surface, newspaper, or folded cloth – scooping out some of the water first will make it much easier to lift the jars from the pan. Tighten the screw-bands on Mason jars, then leave undisturbed for 24 hours, until completely cool. Check the seal the following day (see p. 158).

The oven method

The oven method takes longer than the water bath method, but you can process more jars at a time and don't need to worry about finding a deep pan.

Preheat the oven to 300°F. Stand the jars about 2 inches apart (enough to allow the warm air to circulate) on a thick pad of newspaper, or stand them on newspaper or a folded tea towel in a baking pan filled with water to a depth of $1^1/_4$ inches. Fill the packed jars with boiling syrup and cover with the rubber rings and jar tops, but do not fasten with clips or screw-bands at this stage.

Heat in the oven for the time given in the chart on p. 159. Remove the jars, one at a time, seal with the screw-band or clip immediately, and place on a wooden surface, newspaper, or folded cloth. Leave undisturbed until completely cool, and check the seal the following day (see below).

Testing the seal

It's important to test the seal after canning to be sure that it is absolutely airtight. When the jars are completely cool, undo the clips or remove the screw-bands. Put one hand underneath the jar and, with the other hand, carefully lift the jar by the lid. If it's well sealed, the lid will remain firmly on. You can then refasten the clip or screw-band and put the jar away for storage. If the lid comes away, either reprocess the fruit or eat it up immediately.

Storage

Store canned fruits in a cool, dark, and dry place. They will keep well for up to 1 year. After this, although there may be nothing wrong with them, the texture and color will begin to deteriorate.

Opening jars

The round rubber seal on a lock-lid jar has a small protuberance that should break the seal when pulled. However, it doesn't always work! So for stubborn lock-lid jars and Mason jars, very carefully insert the point of a knife between the rubber ring and the rim and gently lever up. If the seal is still difficult to break, then stand the jar in hot water for a few minutes – this will help to release the seal.

Heating times for water bath and oven canning methods

For safe canning it is important to adhere to these timings. For the water bath method, check the water temperature with a thermometer; for the oven method, preheat the oven and check the temperature using an oven thermometer.

FRUIT	WATER BATH METHOD	OVEN METHOD
Apple slices **Blackberries** **Blueberries** **Currants** **Gooseberries** **Loganberries** **Mulberries** **Raspberries** **Rhubarb** **Strawberries**	Maintain at the simmering point (190°F) for 2 minutes.	• 30–40 minutes for jars below 32 ounces • 45–50 minutes for 32- to 64-ounce jars
Apricots **Cherries** **Plums, whole**	Maintain at the simmering point (190°F) for 10 minutes.	• 40–50 minutes for jars below 32 ounces • 50–60 minutes for 32- to 64-ounce jars
Nectarines **Peaches** **Plums, halved**	Maintain at the simmering point (190°F) for 20 minutes.	• 50–60 minutes for jars below 32 ounces • 60–70 minutes for 32- to 64-ounce jars
Figs **Pears** **Tomatoes, whole**	Maintain at the simmering point (190°F) for 40 minutes.	• 60–70 minutes for jars below 32 ounces • 70–80 minutes for 32- to 64-ounce jars
Fruit purées and pulps (these need to be poured at boiling point into hot jars)	Maintain at the simmering point (190°F) for 5 minutes for fruit pulp, 10 minutes for tomato purée.	Not applicable

Early rhubarb with honey

The arrival of the early, forced rhubarb in January deserves a salutation of the greatest magnitude, and I can never wait to savor its fresh, earthy energy. The blushing stalks, with their tart but delicate flavor, are strictly seasonal, so be sure you don't miss the chance to preserve a jar or two to enjoy later in the year.

Makes two 16-ounce jars
7 tablespoons honey
Juice of 1 large orange (you need 7 tablespoons)
3 pounds, 6 ounces forced rhubarb

Put the honey and 2 cups plus 2 tablespoons of water into a pan and slowly bring to a boil to make a syrup. Remove from the heat and add the orange juice.

Meanwhile, wipe the rhubarb and trim the ends. Cut into even 1- to 2-inch chunks. Place the rhubarb in a bowl and pour in the hot syrup. Let stand for 10 to 12 hours. This soaking makes the rhubarb much easier to pack in the jars.

Using a slotted spoon, take the rhubarb from the syrup and pack into warm, sterilized jars (see p. 152). Bring the syrup to a boil again and pour over the rhubarb, filling the jars to the brim. Cover with lids, remembering to loosen screw-bands, if you're using them, by a quarter of a turn (see p. 156). Stand in a pan with a folded tea towel on the bottom. Cover the jars with warm water (100°F). Bring to the simmering point (190°F) over a period of 25 minutes. Simmer at this temperature for 2 minutes.

Carefully remove the jars from the pan and place on a wooden surface or a folded tea towel. Tighten screw-bands. Leave undisturbed to cool for 24 hours, then check the seals before storing (see p. 158). Use within 1 year.

Variation

Instead of honey and orange juice, try using 2 ounces of very finely sliced fresh ginger and liven up the syrup with ginger cordial or, better still, some ginger wine. Both natives of Asia, ginger and rhubarb are natural partners. So often ingredients that coincide, seasonally or locally, complement each other in the culinary world.

Blues and bay

This recipe, applying the oven method, can be used for preserving the many members of the *Vaccinium* family, which include the cultivated blueberry as well as the wild huckleberry. The delicate, lemony nutmeg note of fresh bay complements their gentle flavor beautifully.

   Serve these fragrant berries for a breakfast treat with thick vanilla yogurt.

Makes three 16-ounce jars

$3/4$ cup superfine sugar

$1/4$ cup lemon juice

$2^1/4$ pounds blueberries or huckleberries

6 fresh bay leaves

Preheat the oven to 300°F.

Start by making a fruit syrup: mix the sugar with $2^1/2$ cups of water in a pan and bring slowly to a boil to dissolve the sugar. Remove from the heat, add the lemon juice, cover, and keep warm.

Pick over the berries, removing any twiggy bits or leaves. Pack them firmly, without crushing, into warm, sterilized jars (see p. 152), sliding the bay leaves attractively around the sides of the jars.

Bring the sugar syrup to a boil and pour over the berries, filling the jars to the brim. Cover with lids, but do not fasten the clips or put on the screw-bands (see p. 158). Put the jars, 2 inches apart, in the oven for 30 minutes.

Carefully remove the jars, seal with screw-bands or clips immediately, and place on a wooden surface, newspaper, or folded cloth. Leave undisturbed until completely cool, and check the seal the following day (see p. 158). Use within 1 year.

Bottled black currants

Season: June to August

The rich, intense flavor of black currants is well preserved by canning, and I find it very useful to have a few jars on the larder shelf. Preserved currants are delicious served with hot steaming custard, vanilla ice cream, or good plain yogurt. When friends drop by, I often open a jar for an instant dessert.

Makes two 16-ounce jars

1 cup granulated sugar
2¹/₂ pounds large, firm, juicy
    black currants

A few lemon verbena or scented
    geranium leaves (optional)

Put the sugar into a pan with 2¹/₂ cups of water and heat gently to dissolve, then boil for 1 minute to make a syrup.

Prepare the black currants by removing any twiggy stems and rinsing the fruit if necessary. Pack the currants as tightly as possible, but without crushing, into warm, sterilized jars (see p. 152). If using verbena or geranium leaves, layer 2 or 3 among the little purple-black fruits as you go.

Cover the packed fruit with the hot syrup (140°F), filling the jars to the brim. Fasten with screw-bands or clips. If using screw-bands, remember to tighten them and then release by a quarter of a turn (see p. 156). Place a folded tea towel in the bottom of a large pan (which must be deeper than your jars are tall). Fill the pan with warm water (100°F), then submerge the jars completely.

Clip a candy thermometer to the side of the pan. Bring the water slowly to the simmering point (190°F) over 25 minutes, then maintain this temperature for just 2 minutes.

Lift the jars out and place on a wooden surface or a folded tea towel. Tighten screw-bands. Leave undisturbed for 24 hours. To check that they are properly sealed, remove the clips or screw-bands and lift the jars by their lids (see p. 158). Store in a cool, dark place. Use within 1 year.

Roasted tomato passata

Season: August to September

For me, tomato passata is an essential pantry ingredient. I use it as a base for my roasted tomato ketchup (see p. 187), as well as for pasta sauces and curries.

The best time to make this preserve is when tomatoes are at their cropping peak – smelling strong, sweet, and aromatic when picked from the vine. This recipe uses $4^1/_2$ pounds of fruit but, if you are using bought tomatoes as opposed to homegrown ones, I suggest you negotiate a good deal with your local grower and buy a boxful or two. You certainly won't regret it. You can't buy passata like this one!

Makes two 16-ounce jars

$4^1/_2$ pounds ripe tomatoes
7 ounces shallots, peeled and
   thinly sliced
3 or 4 garlic cloves, peeled and
   thinly sliced

A few rosemary, thyme, basil,
   or oregano sprigs
1 teaspoon salt
$^1/_2$ teaspoon ground black pepper
1 teaspoon granulated sugar
$^1/_4$ cup olive, sunflower, or canola oil

Preheat the oven to 350°F.

Cut the tomatoes in half and place them, cut side up, in a single layer in a large roasting pan. Scatter the shallots, garlic, herbs, salt, pepper, sugar, and oil over the top. Roast for about 1 hour, until the vegetables are well softened. Remove from the oven and purée with a food mill.

Have your hot, sterilized jars ready (see p. 152). Put the tomato purée into a saucepan and bring to the boiling point. Pour it into the jars, filling them to the brim, and seal immediately with clips or screw-bands. If you're using screw-bands, remember to release the lid by a quarter of a turn (see p. 156).

Stand the jars in a large saucepan with a folded tea towel on the bottom of the pan. Cover with warm water (100°F) and bring to the simmering point (190°F) over a period of 25 minutes, then simmer for 10 minutes.

Remove the jars and stand them on a wooden surface or folded tea towel. Tighten the screw-bands, if using. Leave undisturbed until cool, then check the seal (see p. 158). Use within 1 year. Once opened, refrigerate and use within a few days.

Mulled pears

It always amazes me just how much fruit a gnarled old pear tree can bear in a good season. However, it's still a little tricky to catch pears at their point of perfect ripeness – somewhere between bullet hard and soft and woolly. Never mind, should you find yourself with a boxful of underripe specimens, this recipe turns them into a preserve "pear excellence."

These pears are particularly delicious served with thick vanilla custard or used as a base for a winter fruit salad. Alternatively, try serving them with terrines and pâtés, or mix them with chicory leaves drizzled with a honey mustard dressing and crumbled blue cheese.

Makes two 32-ounce jars
²/₃ **cup granulated sugar**
2 cups cider (dry, medium, or sweet)
3 pounds, 6 ounces small pears

Small handful of cloves
2 (2-inch) pieces of cinnamon stick

Preheat the oven to 300°F.

Start by making a cider syrup: mix the sugar with 2 cups plus 2 tablespoons of water in a pan and bring slowly to a boil to dissolve the sugar. Remove from the heat, add the cider, cover, and keep warm.

Peel the pears, keeping the stems attached. As you do so, place them in a bowl of lightly salted water to stop them from browning. When all the pears are peeled, cut them in half and stud each half with a clove or two. Pack them into warm, sterilized jars (see p. 152), adding a piece of cinnamon to each. Pears are very bottom-heavy, of course, and I find the best way to pack them is head to toe.

Bring the cider syrup to a boil and pour over the pears. Cover the jars with lids, but do not fasten the clips or put on the screw-bands. Place the jars 2 inches apart, in the oven for 1 hour (see p. 158).

Remove the jars, seal with the screw-bands or clips immediately, and place on a wooden surface, newspaper, or folded cloth. Leave undisturbed until completely cool, and check the seal the following day (see p. 158). Use within 1 year.

Variation
Try replacing the cider with red wine, and add a star anise to each jar if you like.

Spiced brandy plums

The Brogdale Trust in Kent is home to the National Fruit Collection – a bit like a Noah's Ark for the fruits of the earth. Among their many living specimens, they grow over 300 different cultivars of *Prunus domestica,* the European plum – also known as dessert plums. These fruits crop from high summer right through into October, giving us plenty to eat fresh, and loads to preserve for later in the year.

In the United States, European plums can be found at farmers' markets, growing in backyards, or at some supermarkets. Or you can preserve peach, nectarine, or apricot halves in the same way.

Makes two 32-ounce jars

$^1/_4$ cup honey

Finely grated zest of 1 orange

7 tablespoons brandy

$2^1/_4$ pounds plums, stems removed

2 cinnamon sticks

2 star anise pods

Start by making a brandy syrup: put the honey and $1^3/_4$ cups of water into a pan, heat gently until the honey is dissolved, then add the orange zest and brandy. Set aside.

Halve the plums lengthwise with a sharp knife. Twist them apart and remove the pit with the point of the knife. Pack the plums into warmed, sterilized jars (see p. 152) with the rounded sides of the fruit following the curve of the jar (you'll fit more in this way). Prod a cinnamon stick and a star anise down the side of each jar.

Pour the hot brandy syrup (140°F) over the fruit until the jars are full to the brim. Tap to remove any air bubbles. Seal with clips or screw-bands, remembering to release the screw-band by a quarter of a turn, if using this type of jar (see p. 156).

Choose a large pan, deep enough for your jars to sit in and be totally immersed in water. Put a folded tea towel on the bottom of the pan and fill with warm water (100°F). Put the jars into the pan, making sure they are completely covered with the water. Bring to the simmering point (190°F) over a period of 25 minutes, then maintain this temperature for 20 minutes.

Transfer the jars to a wooden surface or place on a folded tea towel. Tighten the screw-bands, if using. Leave undisturbed for 24 hours, then check that the seal is secure (see p. 158). Use within 1 year.

Figpote

The fig is a member of the mulberry family and is generally best suited to warmer climates. A contented, well-positioned homegrown tree can crop well, usually in August and September. There are countless varieties, ranging in color from purply black to yellowy green – any can be used for this recipe. Just make sure, when picking or buying, that your figs are ripe, as they do not ripen after picking.

This recipe uses a simplified version of the oven method. Everything is cooked and hot to start with, so it's not necessary to heat the jars for an extended time in the oven. A few jars of these honey-soaked fruits, stored away for the winter months, will be a blissful reminder that the hot days of summer were not just a fig-ment of your imagination. . .

Makes two 8-ounce jars

12 figs (not too big)
²/₃ cup freshly squeezed orange juice

2 cups freshly made Earl Grey
 or green tea
¹/₃ cup honey

Preheat the oven to 275°F and put your sterilized jars (see p. 152) inside to heat.

Wash the figs and remove any hard, twiggy bits of stem – but do not cut right back to the flesh, as this risks splitting the skin.

Put the orange juice, tea, and honey into a pan and gently heat to a simmer to make a syrup. Add the figs and cook gently for 8 to 10 minutes, until tender. Using a slotted spoon, take out the figs and carefully pack them into the hot jars. It may be a bit of a squash, but figs quite like this. Return the filled jars to the oven to keep warm – it is important to keep the jars as hot as possible to create a successful seal.

Bring the fruit syrup to a boil and boil for 6 to 7 minutes to reduce it in volume. Stand the jars on a wooden surface or newspaper and pour the hot syrup over the figs, filling the jars to the brim. Seal immediately with lids, clips, or screw-bands. Leave undisturbed for 24 hours, then check that the seal is secure (see p. 158). Use within 1 year.

Winter fruit compote

Season: winter

It may seem somewhat unnecessary to preserve dried fruit, but I love having a few jars of this compote on the shelf. The once-shriveled fruits become plump and luscious and are quite delicious served alone for breakfast or with yogurt or crème fraîche as a dessert.

I like to make this in early November, when newly dried prunes, figs, and apricots are available. Keep on the lookout for small, dried wild figs, which will plump up perfectly to their original shapely selves. The glistening black prunes from the Agen area in southern France are also key players – I prefer to use these unpitted because they infuse the compote with an almondlike essence.

A simplified version of the oven method is used – everything is cooked and hot to start with, so the jars don't need to be heated for an extended time in the oven.

Makes four 16-ounce jars
3¹/₃ cups dried figs
1¹/₄ cups unsulfured dried apricots
2¹/₃ cups dried prunes, Agen prunes if possible, preferably with pits
4¹/₄ cups freshly made hot green tea, Earl Grey, or breakfast tea
³/₄ cup plus 2 tablespoons freshly squeezed orange juice
7 tablespoons honey

Combine the dried fruit in a large bowl. Pour the hot tea and the orange juice over it and mix together, making sure all the fruit is totally immersed. Cover and let steep for 24 hours.

Preheat the oven to 275°F and place your sterilized jars (see p. 152) inside.

Carefully transfer the fruit and liquid into a large pan. Bring slowly to a simmer on the stovetop and poach the fruit for 10 minutes.

Remove the pan of fruit from the heat. Using a slotted spoon, scoop out the fruit and pack into the hot jars. Return the jars to the oven to keep warm. Add the honey to the steeping juice. Bring to a boil and boil for 5 minutes.

Carefully remove the jars from the oven and pour in the honeyed juice so it comes to the very brim of the jars and completely covers the fruit. Seal immediately with lids, clips, or screw-bands. Leave undisturbed for 24 hours, then check that the seal is secure (see p. 158). Store in a cool, dry place and use within 1 year.

Liz's luscious raspberries

Season: July to late October

This recipe comes from Liz Neville, a virtuoso preserves maker with whom I run the River Cottage Preserved courses. You can make it with any raspberry, but we particularly like to use the big autumn berries. Bottle a few and you can extend your raspberry eating well into the dark winter months.

In an ideal world, the fruit for this preserve would be packed into the jars as you pick it from the canes. That may not be possible – but do make sure the fruit is in tip-top condition and handled as little as possible.

Makes three 16-ounce jars

³/₄ cup granulated sugar
2¹/₄ pounds firm, just-ripe raspberries

¹/₂ to ²/₃ cup brandy, gin,
    vodka, or raspberry liqueur

First make a syrup: put the sugar and 3¹/₄ cups of water into a pan and heat slowly to dissolve the sugar, then bring to a boil. Keep the syrup warm.

Pack the raspberries tightly into warm, sterilized jars (see p. 152). Make sure you don't bruise the fruit – a chopstick or wooden spoon handle is useful for gently prodding it down. Pour the alcohol over the packed fruit. Fill the jars to the brim with the sugar syrup, tapping them to remove any air bubbles. Put the lids on the jars, loosening screw-bands by a quarter of a turn, if you're using them, to allow the steam to escape (see p. 156).

Stand the jars in a deep pan and cover with warm water (100°F). Heat to the simmering point (190°F) over 25 minutes. Maintain this temperature for 2 minutes.

Carefully remove the jars and stand them on a wooden surface or thick folded towel. Tighten the screw-bands, then leave the jars undisturbed to cool. When cool, check the seal by removing the clips or screw-bands and lifting the jars by the lid (see p. 158). Use within 1 year.

Quince and apple sauce

Season: September to October

The raw flesh of the lumpy yellow quince is dry and disagreeably sour. However, once cooked, it becomes pink and highly perfumed. Lightly sweetened and combined with good fluffy cooking apples, such as Granny Smiths, it makes a delightful accompaniment for roast pork or duck. I also love this aromatic fruity sauce on a home-baked rice pudding.

Makes four 8-ounce jars

1 pound, 2 ounces quince, peeled, cored, and chopped

Juice of $^1/_2$ lemon

1 pound, 2 ounces cooking apples, peeled, cored, and chopped

$^2/_3$ cup granulated sugar

Put the quince, lemon juice, and 2 cups plus 2 tablespoons of water into a saucepan. Bring to a boil, then simmer for 8 to 10 minutes (quince takes longer to soften than apple and needs a bit of a head start). Add the apples and sugar and cook for a further 10 to 15 minutes, until all the fruit is well softened. Remove from the heat and either beat to a smooth pulp with a wooden spoon or press through a sieve.

Meanwhile, preheat the oven to 275°F and place the sterilized jars (see p. 152) inside.

Return the pulp to the pan and bring to a boil, stirring to make sure it doesn't stick and burn. Remove from the heat and pour immediately into the warm, sterilized jars. Seal with lids, clips, or screw-bands, remembering to release the screw-band by a quarter of a turn if using this type of jar (see p. 156). Place in a deep pan with a folded tea towel on the bottom. Cover with warm water (100°F), bring to the simmering point (190°F), then simmer for 5 minutes.

Remove the jars from the hot water and place on a wooden surface or folded tea towel. Tighten the screw-bands, if using, and leave the jars undisturbed until cool. Check the seal (see p. 158). Store in a cool, dry place. Use within 1 year.

Sauces, Ketchups & Oil-based Preserves

Sauces, pastes, and condiments are among the

tasty recipes in this chapter. Vinegar, sugar, salt, and oil all come into play as preservatives; you will find more detailed information on these ingredients on pp. 27–31. Oil has been used as an air-excluding ingredient since ancient times to keep foods from spoiling. With the increasing availability of superb-quality oils, this is a delicious and luxurious way of preserving. It is certainly a branch of preserving that I find very exciting and rewarding. This chapter will introduce you to the following range of preserves.

Sauces This is a generic term if ever there was one, but for the purposes of this book, I define a sauce as a smooth condiment generally made with similar ingredients to a chutney (see p. 86). The cooked, spiced fruits and vegetables are either sieved or puréed to give a thick, pourable consistency.

Ketchups Sometimes referred to in old recipe books as catsups or catchups, these are generally thinner than sauces and made from a single fruit or vegetable with vinegar and seasonings.

Vegetables in oil The technique of using oil to preserve lightly blanched or brined vegetables is strongly associated with Mediterranean countries, where olive oil is abundant. It is particularly suited to vegetables with strong flavors, such as globe artichokes, asparagus, dried tomatoes, and mushrooms – not least because they will flavor the oil, which can also be used.

Pestos and pastes These intense condiments are made from aromatic or strongly spiced ingredients and do not contain high levels of salt, vinegar, or other preservatives. For this reason, they need to be sealed off from the air with a layer of oil and refrigerated, and generally should not be kept for more than a month or two. After some has been taken from the jar, the oil covering should always be replaced, which may mean topping with a little more.

Flavored oils Easily made by steeping herbs, spices, or other robustly flavored ingredients in oil, these are among the simplest and most rewarding of preserves to make. They enliven everything from salad dressings and mayonnaise to marinades and stir-fries. Use warm oil for firm ingredients such as chiles and spices, and cold oil for green herbs.

Coulis Made from very lightly sweetened fruit that is simply sieved or puréed, coulis are usually based on juicy summer berries and currants.

Garden pesto

Season: July to August

The big, platelike leaves of the nasturtium plant (*Tropaeolum majus*) are abundant throughout the summer and often well into the golden months of autumn. With their peppery flavor, they make the perfect base for a fiery pesto. Add a sprig or two of garden mint, a few golden marigold petals, and some spicy nasturtium seeds and you have a wonderful sauce to stir into pasta, swirl on soups, or just smear in a sandwich. Pick the leaves on a warm, dry day – ideally, earlier in the summer, before the caterpillars have decided to feast on them.

Whenever I make pesto, I replace the traditional Parmesan with a hard goat's cheese, matured for a year. It makes an excellent alternative to Parmesan in all kinds of dishes.

Makes about three 4-ounce jars

2 ounces nasturtium leaves
2 or 3 mint leaves (optional)
2 garlic cloves, peeled and crushed
6 or so nasturtium seed pods (see p. 103)
6 tablespoons pine nuts (optional)
2^1/$_2$ ounces mature, hard goat's cheese or Parmesan, finely grated

^{1}/$_4$ cup lemon juice
^{2}/$_3$ cup hempseed, canola, or olive oil, plus extra to seal
Petals from 2 marigold flowers
Salt to taste

Purists say that pesto should be made by pounding the ingredients together using a mortar and pestle. For this recipe, you can certainly do that, starting by crushing the nasturtium leaves, mint leaves (if using), garlic, nasturtium pods, and nuts, then adding the cheese, followed by the lemon juice and oil. Pound until well blended, folding in the marigold petals and salt at the very end.

Then again, you can do as I do and simply whiz everything (except the marigold petals and salt) in a food processor for a couple of minutes until you have a soft, well-blended mixture. Remove from the processor and fold in the petals and salt.

(continued)

Either way, spoon the pesto into small, sterilized jars (see p. 21) and pour a little oil over the surface to exclude any air. Cap with metal lids (see p. 22). Store in the fridge and use within 1 month. If you are making a lot of pesto, pack in small containers and freeze.

When you come to use the pesto, stir it well before spooning out. Make sure the surface of any pesto remaining in the jar is completely covered with oil before you return it to the fridge (this is very important if it is to keep well).

Variations

Traditionally, pesto is made with the leaves of the sweet basil plant (*Ocimum basilicum*). If you manage to grow it in good quantities, do make use of it in this recipe. Alternatively, try some other herbs as the base for your pesto. Young, raw nettle tops and wild garlic leaves (both to be gathered in early spring) work beautifully together; parsley (flat-leaf or curly) also works well. Hazels or walnuts can stand in for pine nuts, and a mature, robust Cheddar is a good alternative to Parmesan.

P.S. *Calendula officinalis*, or common garden marigold, is a really useful herb and should not be ignored for culinary purposes. The golden pigment of the petals can be used, like saffron, to color rice, cakes, desserts, and butter. Alternatively, sprinkle the bittersweet, aromatic petals over mixed salad greens, or toss a few into a fresh herb omelet.

Slow-dried tomatoes in oil

Season: July to September

I love the gutsy flavor of these tomatoes and like to serve them as part of a crisp smoked bacon and beet salad or a hearty couscous salad with plenty of fresh cilantro. There are times, though, when I can't resist eating them from the jar!

Ideally, the fruit would be sun-dried, but slowly drying them in a very low oven achieves similar and very pleasing results.

Makes three to five 4-ounce jars

4¹/₂ pounds tomatoes

2 teaspoons salt

2 teaspoons granulated sugar

7 tablespoons white wine vinegar

³/₄ to 1¹/₂ cups olive, canola, or sunflower oil

Preheat the oven to 200° to 225°F. Cut the tomatoes in half around their middles and scoop out the seeds with a teaspoon. Put the tomatoes, cut sides up, on a wire rack with a baking sheet underneath to catch any drips. Sprinkle a few grains of salt and sugar on each cut tomato half. Leave for 10 to 15 minutes for the seasoning to begin to permeate the tomato flesh, then turn the tomatoes so their cut sides face down on the rack.

Set the rack of tomatoes atop the baking sheet in the oven and leave them to dry for 6 to 10 hours; the drying time will depend on their size and juiciness. The tomatoes are ready when they are dry to the touch but still a little plump and fleshy. They'll have reduced by about 90 percent, and the total weight after drying will be about 7 ounces. Don't let the tomatoes dry until they become brittle. Remove from the oven and allow to cool, then transfer to a shallow dish. Pour the vinegar over the tomatoes, cover, and let stand for about 30 minutes.

Pack the tomatoes into sterilized jars (see p. 21) to within ³/₄ inch of the top of the jars. Distribute the vinegar between the jars and then cover the tomatoes completely with the oil, tapping the jars to expel any trapped air. Seal with lids (see p. 22). Store in a cool, dry place and use within 4 months. Once opened, store in the fridge, always make sure the tomatoes are fully covered with oil, and use within 6 weeks.

Variations
Use half balsamic and half white wine vinegar if you prefer. A tablespoonful or two of finely chopped preserved lemons (p. 118) is a flavorful addition.

Roasted tomato ketchup

Season: July to September

Slow-roasted tomatoes provide a rich, intense base for this, my all-time favorite ketchup. The spices and seasonings I have used are good old-fashioned ones – those our grandmothers would have kept in their kitchens. However, if you like, you can fire it up by adding a couple of teaspoonfuls of ground chiles. Don't expect the ketchup to be the same color as a commercial variety; it will be a warm orangey red color.

Makes 2 to 2¹/₂ cups

4¹/₄ cups roasted tomato
    passata (p. 165)
7 tablespoons cider vinegar
¹/₄ cup lemon juice
1 heaping teaspoon celery salt

1 heaping teaspoon English mustard
    powder (see p. 202)
1 heaping teaspoon ground ginger
¹/₂ teaspoon ground black pepper
¹/₄ teaspoon ground cloves
¹/₂ cup Demerara sugar

Put the passata into a heavy pan with the vinegar, lemon juice, and spices. Bring to a simmer, then add the sugar. Stir until dissolved, then continue to simmer, stirring occasionally, for 25 to 30 minutes, until the sauce is reduced to a thick but pourable consistency.

Pour immediately into warm, sterilized bottles or jars (see p. 152). Seal immediately with vinegar-proof lids (see p. 22). Store in a cool, dry place and use within 4 months. For longer keeping, sterilize the filled jars using the method on p. 125. Once opened, keep in the fridge.

Variation

Rhubarb makes a delightful fruity ketchup; this is a good way to use up the tougher, tarter stalks toward the end of the rhubarb season. Slow roast 4¹/₂ pounds of chopped rhubarb with 9 ounces of chopped red onions and 3 or 4 garlic cloves at 350°F for about 1 hour. Strain through a sieve and put into a heavy saucepan. Use the same quantities of sugar and vinegar as above, but leave out the lemon juice (as rhubarb is very acidic). Replace the mustard, black pepper, and cloves with a good teaspoonful each of ground cumin and coriander. Continue to cook as for tomato ketchup.

Harissa paste

Season: July to September

Harissa is a North African ingredient used to enhance many fish and meat dishes, as well as couscous and soups. I also like to use my version to make a fruity, fiery dipping sauce (see below) to serve with pork, fish, or prawns.

The strength of the paste depends on the variety and quantity of chiles used. The chances are that this recipe, which I would describe as moderately hot, will merely tickle the palate of out-and-out chile freaks. But all you need do to make it more fiery is increase the amount of chiles, include more of their seeds (see below), or perhaps add one or two very hot little dried chiles.

Makes about ³/₄ cup

9 ounces tomatoes	1 teaspoon caraway seeds
2 ounces hot chiles	1 teaspoon coriander seeds
2 fat garlic cloves	¹/₂ teaspoon salt
2 ounces shallots	¹/₄ cup olive or hempseed oil

Drop the tomatoes into a pan of boiling water for 30 seconds, then scoop out and peel off the skins.

Remove the stems from the chiles. The seeds contain most of the fruit's heat, and at this point, you can choose to either leave all the seeds in or, for a less intense paste, cut some of them out. Make sure you wash your hands after handling chiles and avoid touching your eyes for awhile, as the chile oil will burn them.

Put the skinned tomatoes, chiles, and all the other ingredients except the oil in a food processor and process until well blended. Pour into a small saucepan and heat until boiling, then simmer for about 10 minutes, until reduced and starting to thicken. Let cool, then pack into warm, sterilized jars (see p. 21), leaving a ³/₈-inch gap at the top. Pour oil over the paste to completely cover it. Seal the jars.

Store in the fridge and use within 4 months. If you want to extend the shelf life, pack in small, sealable containers and freeze. Once opened, keep in the fridge, making sure the paste in the jar is completely covered by a layer of oil.

P.S. For a tasty chile plum dipping sauce, simmer ¹/₄ cup of rice vinegar or cider vinegar, 5 tablespoons of plum jam (p. 61), and 1 teaspoon of harissa paste until reduced and thickened.

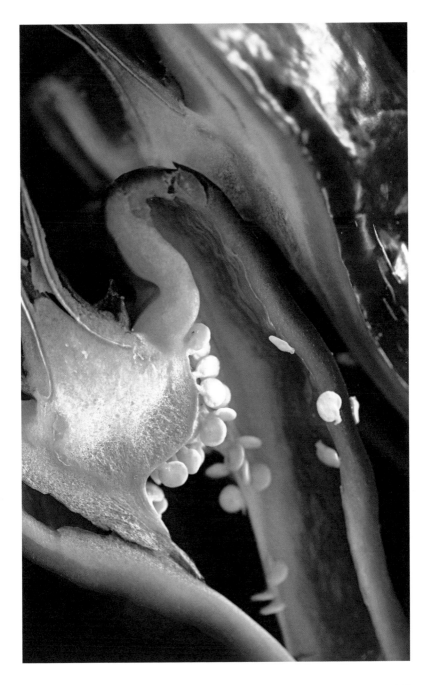

Asparagus preserved in oil

Season: May to June

Spotting the first tips of asparagus pushing their way aboveground in late spring is one of the greatest moments of the growing year.

Use a good but not really expensive olive oil (see p. 30). When the asparagus has been eaten, the flavored oil can be used to make a lovely salad dressing.

You will need one jam jar that is about 8 inches high, with a capacity of about 16 ounces, and a second jar with a capacity of about 8 ounces.

Makes 2 jars (one 16-ounce, one 8-ounce)

1 pound, 2 ounces asparagus	1 teaspoon peppercorns
1¼ cups cider vinegar or white wine vinegar	A few rosemary, thyme, or basil sprigs
2 fat garlic cloves or shallots, finely sliced	7 tablespoons lemon juice
	1¾ to 2 cups olive oil

Trim away the tough woody ends of the asparagus, then cut into lengths ⅜ inch less than the height of your larger jar, keeping the tender trimmed-off bits to one side.

Put the vinegar and about ¾ cup of water in a saucepan and bring to a boil. Remove from the heat and cover to keep warm. Meanwhile, place a griddle pan over high heat. Add the long asparagus spears and cook, turning once or twice, until lightly charred. Drop the spears into the hot vinegar bath and leave for 3 to 4 minutes. This sharpens the flavor of the asparagus, while the acidity assists in preventing bacterial growth.

Put about two-thirds of the garlic or shallots and peppercorns in the sterilized 16-ounce jar (see p. 21). Remove the asparagus from the vinegar bath and pack it, upright, into the jar. Add a few herbs. Pour in two-thirds of the lemon juice, then cover completely with oil. Seal with a lid (see p. 22). Repeat the entire process with the trimmed-off ends and the smaller jar, using up the remaining garlic, peppercorns, herbs, lemon juice, and oil.

Keep in a cool, dark place for 6 weeks before using. Consume within 4 months. Once opened, keep in the fridge, making sure the asparagus in the jar remains covered with oil, and use within 6 weeks.

Variations
Substitute char-grilled peppers or lightly cooked artichoke hearts for the asparagus.

SAUCES, KETCHUPS & OIL-BASED PRESERVES   191

Flavored oils

Season: more or less anytime

These are dead easy to make and have endless applications in the kitchen. Use them to baste or brown ingredients and they will add pizzazz and excitement to stews and roasts. Likewise, they will jazz up a panful of onions or other vegetables for a soup or sauce and impart character to fish dishes. Herb oils come into their own when drizzled over summer or winter salads; they are also excellent used in mayonnaises and dressings.

The basic principle is to choose robust flavorings and leave them for long enough to impart their mighty characters to the oil. Always use a good-quality oil as your base (see pp. 30–31). In all cases, to prevent the oil from becoming rancid, store in a cool place and use within 6 months.

Chile oil

Split open 6 to 8 dried or fresh chiles. Pack into a dry, sterilized 16- to 20-ounce jar or bottle (see p. 152), along with 1 teaspoon of black peppercorns. Heat 2 cups plus 2 tablespoons of olive or canola oil to about 104°F and pour over the chiles. Cover and leave to infuse for 14 days – a little more for a stronger oil. Strain and rebottle.

Nice spice oil

In a dry frying pan, heat 1 tablespoon each of coriander, cumin, and fennel seeds together with a couple of dried chiles. Toast until they release their distinctive fragrances and just start to brown – shake the pan frequently to prevent them from burning. Crush the toasted seeds, then transfer them to a dry, sterilized 16- to 20-ounce jar or bottle (see p. 152). Pour in 2 cups plus 2 tablespoons of canola oil. Store for a couple of weeks before straining the oil and rebottling.

Herb oil

Lightly pack a dry, sterilized 20-ounce jar (see p. 152) with freshly gathered herbs such as basil, rosemary, thyme, sage, or oregano. You can use individual herbs on their own or mix a few together. Pour in 2 cups plus 2 tablespoons of olive oil and store in a cool place for a couple of weeks before straining and rebottling the oil.

Pontack (elderberry) sauce

Season: August to September

This is kitchen alchemy at its most exciting and rewarding: a mysterious-looking brew of dark elderberries, vinegar, and spices becomes a truly wonderful sauce, a secret weapon for the pantry that I don't like to be without. According to tradition, pontack sauce is best used after 7 years, but I'm hard pushed to keep it for 7 months. Pungent, fruity, and spicy, it's an unrivaled partner for winter stews, slow-roasted pork belly, or anything wild and gamy. Besides serving this sauce alongside meat dishes, you can add a couple of tablespoonfuls to sauces and gravies.

The elderberry season is short and the berries are part of the hedgerow banquet for woodland birds, so don't delay – gather them when you see them.

Makes one 12-ounce bottle

1 pound, 2 ounces elderberries	4 allspice berries
2 cups plus 2 tablespoons cider vinegar	1 blade of mace
7 ounces shallots, peeled and sliced	1 tablespoon black peppercorns
6 cloves	$^1/_2$ ounce fresh ginger, bruised

Strip the berries from the stems as soon as possible after picking – a table fork is useful for doing this. Place the berries in an ovenproof earthenware or glass dish with the vinegar and put in a very low oven (about 250°F) for 4 to 6 hours, or overnight. Remove from the oven and strain through a sieve, crushing the berries with a potato masher as you do so to obtain maximum juice.

Put the rich, red-black juice in the pan along with the sliced shallots, cloves, allspice, mace, peppercorns, and ginger. Bring to a gentle boil and cook for 20 to 25 minutes, until slightly reduced (perhaps muttering some magic charm while you watch over the dark, bubbling potion). Remove from the heat and strain through a sieve.

Return the juice to the pan and bring to a boil, then boil steadily for 5 minutes. Pour the sauce into a warm, sterilized bottle (see p. 152) and seal (see p. 22). Store in a cool, dark cupboard.

P.S. This sauce grows better with age, so try to lay some bottles down for a few months if you can.

Saucy haw ketchup

Season: September to December

Hawthorn is a lovely tree that grows throughout the United States. Frothy white blossoms herald the beginning of summer, and the fading flowers later give way to clusters of blood-red berries, or haws. These swathe the trees from early autumn well into winter – sometimes even through to the new year. The peppery, lemony little berries are too tart to eat raw, but I love them cooked into this sweet-sour sauce.

Hawthorn tends to fruit prolifically, so you should have little trouble gathering enough haws. Do avoid picking from roadside bushes, however, as these may have absorbed fumes and pollution (although, for some reason, they often seem to be laden with the biggest and juiciest berries of all!).

Serve haw ketchup with rich meats such as venison or slow-roasted pork belly. It is also terrific drizzled over Welsh rarebit. My favorite way to enjoy this spicy sauce, however, is with a really good nut roast, served with a crisp green salad.

Makes one 10-ounce bottle

1 pound, 2 ounces haws
1^1/$_4$ cups white wine vinegar or
   cider vinegar

^{3}/$_4$ cup plus 1 tablespoon
   granulated sugar
^{1}/$_2$ teaspoon salt
Ground black pepper to taste

Strip the haws from the stems – the easiest way to do this is to snip them off with a pair of scissors or pruning shears. Rinse in cold water.

Put the haws into a pan with the vinegar and 1^1/$_4$ cups of water and simmer for about 30 minutes – the skins will split, revealing the firm, yellow flesh. Cook until the flesh is soft and the berries have become a muted red-brown. Remove from the heat. Press the mixture through a sieve or pass through a food mill to remove the largish seeds and the skins.

Return the fruity mixture to the cleaned-out pan. Add the sugar and heat gently, stirring, until it dissolves. Bring to a boil and cook for 5 minutes. Season with the salt and pepper. Pour into a sterilized bottle (see p. 152) and seal with a vinegar-proof cap (see p. 22). Use within 1 year.

Souper mix

Season: more or less anytime

A good vegetable bouillon or stock can be the making of many a soup, risotto, or sauce. Preparing your own stock from scratch is easy enough – but it does take a little time, so an instant alternative is often welcome. The choice of vegetable bouillon powders and stock cubes on the market is pretty limited. There are one or two good products, but if you use them frequently, you might find an underlying uniformity creeping into your cooking. This is my solution. Whip up your very own souper mix – a concentrated paste of fresh vegetables simply preserved with salt. It's quick and easy to make and the stock it produces is delicious.

You can use just about any herbs or vegetables you like – the important thing is that they are fresh and taste as *vegetable-y* as possible. My preferred ingredients are indicated in this recipe, but you could also use young turnips, shallots, celery, rutabagas, beets, or peppers, as well as bay leaves, thyme, lovage, or mint – almost anything, really. Just bear in mind that the character of the stock will vary depending on the ingredients you choose.

The following are prepared weights; i.e., the ingredients should be washed, trimmed, and peeled (where necessary).

Makes three to four 8-ounce jars

9 ounces leek	2 or 3 garlic cloves
7 ounces fennel	3¹/₂ ounces parsley
7 ounces carrot	3¹/₂ ounces cilantro
9 ounces celery root	³/₄ cup plus 1 tablespoon salt
2 ounces sun-dried tomatoes	

The helping hand of a food processor is essential in this recipe. Simply put all the ingredients into the processor and blend together. The result will be a moist, granular paste. Spoon into sterilized jars (see p. 21) and seal with vinegar-proof lids (see p. 22).

Keep one jar of the mix in the fridge – within easy reach for everyday cooking. The rest can be stored in a cool, dark, and dry place. Use within 6 months.

To use souper mix, just stir about 1 teaspoon of it into 1 cup of hot water.

Notes to the
U.S. Edition

Notes to the U.S. edition

In editing this book for an American audience, we sought to do two things: (1) to make it as much a treasure trove of information, inspiration, and solid cooking guidance for Americans as it is for its original British audience; and (2) to retain Pam Corbin's engaging style. To that end, the recipes and cooking instructions, as well as the information about ingredients and equipment, have been Americanized, so that the ingredients, terminology, and measurements are familiar to U.S. readers. We've made our best attempt to address these particulars. Any errors or omissions are that of the American publisher, Ten Speed Press.

All recipe yields are stated in fluid ounces. Yields and jar sizes are as close as possible to the original, but if you have a bit of preserves left over after packing, you can refrigerate and use in the short term (within a couple of weeks).

English mustard is hotter than the mustard normally found in the United States. English mustard powder can be found in the U.S. in gourmet food stores and specialty shops, and online.

Rosehips are the orange-red fruit of the rose. Rosehips from the wild rose or dog rose seem to have a better flavor than those from cultivated roses. However, some garden varieties of rose also produce cookable hips—notably, *Rosa rugosa*. If you want to harvest rosehips from your garden, do not deadhead your roses.

There are so many different types of plums (over 300 in the UK alone) that most of the plum recipes should adapt easily to using a different variety. However, it should be noted that Japanese plums (large, round, juicy) are the most common plums found in U.S. supermarkets, while European plums (*Prunus domestica*) and American native plums (such as the beach plum) are usually smaller, oval, and more dense. Wild damsons and sloes are subspecies of the European plum that are usually too bitter to eat raw. If you are substituting plums that are quite sweet, you will want to reduce the amount of sugar in the recipe.

Acknowledgments

When asked if I would write this book, I hadn't realized just how many waking (and nighttime) moments my thoughts would invariably be stuck in some form of jam jar or another. It's been a huge privilege, giving me the opportunity to adventure into new, exciting, and often stirring territories, all contained in the amazing world of preserving. However, it would not have been possible for me to do so without the immeasurable help and support of family, friends, and acquaintances, who have journeyed with me, solidly supporting me throughout.

First and foremost, heartfelt thanks to Gavin Kingcome for his stunning photography, bringing ingredients and recipes alive, and for his steady patience on our photo shoot days. Also to Nikki Duffy for her thorough attention to detail in checking recipes, thus reinforcing your success and victory in the jam pan.

Thank you to friends and neighbors in and around the Uplyme Valleys for their open generosity in allowing me to beg and sometimes steal produce from over the garden wall. I would particularly like to thank John and Henriette Wood for giving me a free rein to visit Rhode Hill Gardens – its rich biodiversity quite the highlight of photo shoot days.

On the technical front, thanks to Liz Neville for her invaluable fund of preserving knowledge, and to the outstanding technical team at Wilkin & Sons Ltd.

My thanks to the thoughtful and brilliant Bloomsbury team: Richard Atkinson, Natalie Hunt, and Erica Jarnes, along with Will Webb for his outstanding work and ideas on the layout. Sincere thanks also to gifted editor Janet Illsley, who meticulously and with great calm has perfectly potted, packed, and sealed the book.

Thank you to Trisha Bye for keeping my kitchen and jam jars in apple pie order and to her daughter Sophie for her jammy creativeness. Thanks also to Lois Wakeman for her on the spot availability for eleventh-hour photography.

At home, thank you to my husband Hugh for his support at all times, particularly for his lack of complaint when I dropped a full 2-liter bottle of his amazingly good sloe gin, and to Pip and Maddy, who have never faltered with their help, advice, and enthusiasm, and have seemingly always shared family life with a ton or two of jam.

A big thank-you to Rob Love and the River Cottage team for their confidence that I could write the book. And last, but by no means least, immense thanks to Hugh Fearnley-Whittingstall, warrior and leader of the seasonal and local revolution. Long may it last!

Index